Midwest Gem, Fossil and Mineral Trails
Great Lakes States

Minnesota, Wisconsin, Indiana, Illinois, Michigan, Ohio

by
June Culp Zeitner

$5.95

Gem Guides Book Company
3677 San Gabriel Parkway
Pico Rivera, California 90660

Library of Congress Catalogue Number 88-81986

ISBN 0-935182-39-X

Maps: *JEAN HAMMOND*

Note: Due to the possibility of misinterpretation of information, *Midwest Gem, Fossil and Mineral Trails–Great Lakes States*, its author, publisher and all other persons directly or indirectly involved with this publication assume no responsibility for accidents, injury or any losses by individuals or groups using this publication.

In rough terrain and hazardous areas all persons are advised to be aware of the possible changes due to man or nature that can occur along the gem trails.

Table of Contents

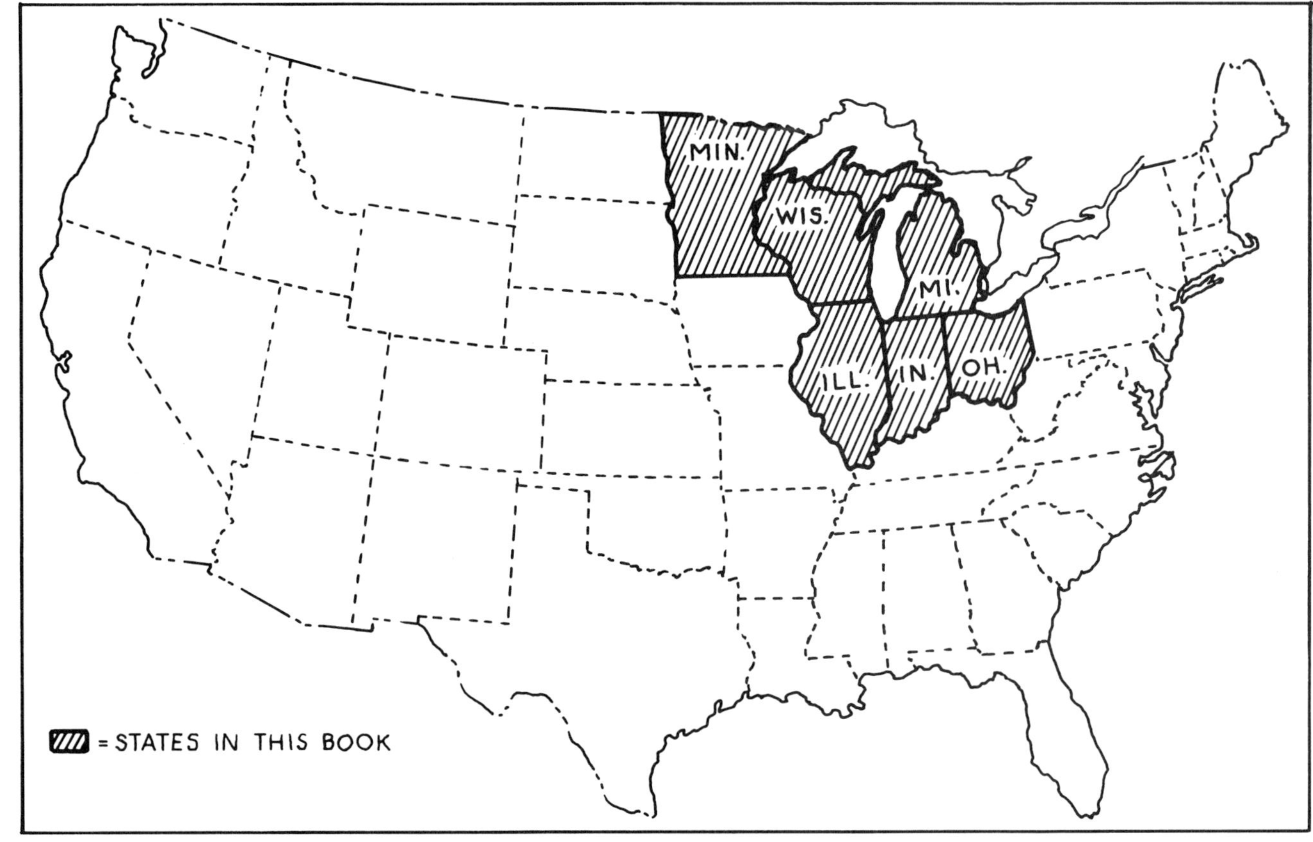
MIN.
WIS.
MI.
ILL.
IN.
OH.
= STATES IN THIS BOOK

ACKNOWLEDGEMENTS

Although I have personally visited most of these states many times, and have collected at numerous well-known sites, it is impossible for one person to keep up with the fast changing scene. This is a large area with hundreds of opportunities for gem, mineral and fossil hobbyists. I treasure the fine specimens from these localities which I have in my collection, but I treasure even more the generous and wonderful people in these states who have helped me with this book. By conversation and by letter many have given me late and pertinent information. I am indebted to many, but particularly the following: Hazel Kunz, Don Auler, Jean Reynolds, Tom Weisner, Joe Claxton, Charlotte Charno, Francis Balsford, Lewis Kehr, Dr. Benjamin Moulton, Carol Anderson, Lloyd Brown, Klaus Westphal, Kitty and Marve Starbuck, Stan Franczak, Bob Williams, Richard Whiteman, Robert Beauvais and Harold McClure. My thanks to each of them for all they have done to make the earth science hobbies so vital in the Great Lakes States of the Midwest. Thanks too to the clubs, museums, scientists and dealers who work to increase our knowledge and enjoyment of this great hobby. I also wish to thank the land owners, mine and quarry operators and others who allow us to contribute to science by collecting. Thanks too to my husband Albert who led me into the world of rocks and has been patient and helpful when the typewriter stole my time.

FOREWORD

Recent changes in field trip availability in the Midwest create many problems for the collector. Many formerly excellent collecting sites have been withdrawn because of reclamation projects in old mining areas, because new construction covers up old sites, or because quarries or mines have changed hands. Large construction companies which operate in many states are not as likely to grant permission to collect as the former locally owned companies. In some cases regulation and insurance costs make it difficult for quarries to allow visitors. And, of course, many once productive areas are depleted. Carelessness and vandalism, mostly on the part of people not involved in the gem hobby, have caused numerous closings. The Bureau of Land Management and Forest Service rules have also changed; access roads are closed off. In all it seems that today's hobbyists have nowhere to start.

On the other hand, new discoveries are being made each year; exploration for mineral resources continues with the aid of satellites. Metal detectors are now used more often by field collectors, giving them a new edge. Other collectors are out collecting by boat or scuba diving equipment.

Most of the Midwest is private property so materials may be found in formerly productive areas almost anywhere permission to collect can be obtained.

There are miles and miles of beaches on the Great Lakes and other glacial lakes, along man-made reservoirs, and along the many rivers and streams of this region where agates, fossils, and minerals can be found. In recent years the largest Lake Superior agate ever reported was found in Minnesota, and new species of fossils have been collected in Illinois, Indiana, and Michigan. Dow Chemical has reported finding diamonds in the kimberlites of upper Michigan, and vast mineral deposits were located in northern Wisconsin. The Great Lakes States of the Midwest still have abundant resources, and those who collect for a hobby can still be rewarded for their

Some clubs have been actively working to reopen closed sites or to develop new areas. By working together clubs in most districts continue to have productive field trips. Most clubs welcome visitors, and many clubs sponsor periodic trips where visitors can join club members. Such trips may be in connection with annual shows or rock swaps.

Our hobby, collecting earth science materials and using them for educational or artistic purposes, is fairly new as hobbies go. Our success at collecting depends on our good name and our public relations.

Guided by the Golden Rule and the AFMS Code of Ethics, as well as by old-fashioned common sense, every collector should be a goodwill ambassador to help assure the future success and growth of the hobby.

HOW TO USE THIS BOOK

This book is a guide to hundreds of collecting areas, but it cannot give you a guarantee that you will be able to get in when you get to the destination of your choice. You will have to get specific permission on each trip. Although many of these spots give you specific directions, you may have better luck with the more general information. When exact spots are given they tend to be depleted faster and closed off sooner. The informed collector should learn the geology, mineralogy and paleontology of an area and look for similar outcrops to the better known sites. The expert collector will also learn to work a little harder, dig a little deeper, work more carefully, and stay at it longer than in previous times.

Any collector going on a trip very far from home should make every effort to get all possible recent information before making that trip. Land status is constantly changing. By phone or by letter, lots of current information is available. Following are some helps in preparing for a successful trip.

1. Contact rock clubs in the area you propose to visit.
2. Write to the Chambers of Commerce, the State Geological Surveys, the State Divisions of Tourism, to museums, mining companies, fee basis operators, listed guides or any other place

from which you think you might be able to get information. Not all will answer, but enough will so that you can know what to do next.

3. Send for detailed topographical maps. Index maps of the United States Geological Survey are free. Write the United States Geological Survey, 1220 Sunrise Valley Drive, Reston, Virginia 22092.
4. Keep up with articles in hobby magazines.
5. Subscribe to club bulletins of the area you are most interested in.
6. Look up the names of rock shops of the area which you are interested in and order samples of local specimens by mail so you can study the items you hope to look for. Becoming a mail order customer of the shop may help you get collecting information when you go to the shop in person.
7. There are guide books or specific publications for many of the states. Some guide books may be for one area or for one type of field trip, for example invertebrate fossils or guide books for scenic sites of geological interest. Read anything you can about an area.
8. If you have adequate safety equipment and a comprehensive liability insurance policy, it can be easier to get permission to collect.
9. It is helpful to plan trips to coincide with local shows.
10. Members of the club nearest to you may have taken trips to the sites you wish to visit. Join and support your local club. Members may be able to help you get the information you are seeking.
11. Don't leave things to chance. Plan the important part of your trip before you go.

The individual state maps have the counties marked where gems, minerals and fossils have been found. While gem occurrences are given priority, fossil and mineral sites are not neglected.

Counties in the northern part of each state are given first. The states start with the farthest west, Minnesota, and move in sequence to the farthest east, Ohio.

HOW TO HUNT GEMS, MINERALS, AND FOSSILS IN THE MIDWEST

The Midwest is used as a rather general term by the media. Eastern writers and television anchors conceive of it as starting just west of New York state and reaching to the Rocky Mountains. For this book the Midwest includes the Great Lakes states west of New York. All six of these states with

Great Lakes shoreline are east of the Mississippi except for Minnesota, where the Mississippi originates in the northcentral part of the state and does not become the state border until it is south of St. Paul. Minnesota is a Lake Superior State. Wisconsin has shoreline on both Lake Superior and Lake Michigan. Michigan is the state with the most shoreline on these vast inland fresh water seas, with waters of Lake Superior, Michigan and Huron virtually surrounding it. Illinois and Indiana are bordered in part by Lake Michigan, and Ohio hugs the edge of Lake Erie.

These states were all glaciated, and all have great rivers and valleys. Limestone built up from ancient seas is the common surface rock, but there are also sands, clays and igneous intrusions. The mineral resources include copper, iron, lead, zinc, silver, gold, coal, gravel, clay, quartz, gypsum, granite, salt, and more.

Climate is an important factor for collectors. These states are all subject to sudden extremes; rainfall, snow, and winds are common along the lakes. Summers are warm and humid. Most residents prefer collecting in the spring or fall. Tornadoes and severe storms are possible in any of these states. The cool summer spots are the north shore of Lake Superior in Minnesota, and the Keweenaw peninsula of Michigan. Southern Illinois, southern Indiana and southern Ohio have milder winters than the rest of the area.

Wherever you travel in the Midwest be prepared for any kind of weather. Sturdy clothing of cotton denim is a good choice. Layered with a wool sweater and a windbreaker, such an outfit is good over a wide range of temperature. Comfortable well-built shoes or boots are a must. Safety shoes are required in some quarries and are sensible for mine dumps too. Safety goggles are also a requirement for admission in some places because they are such excellent protection for the eyes from flying bits of rock. An eye shade is helpful if the sun is bright. Admission may not be granted if you do not have a hardhat.

Clothes with plenty of pockets are handy for collectors where you can store notebook, pencil, tissues, plastic bags, small tools, a canteen of water and an orange or chocolate bar.

There are many more places to collect in the six states than are mentioned in this book. But the book seeks to help you find many places with the leads provided.

Ask to look at farmers' stone piles amassed from glacial rocks scattered in their fields. Stop and look at road cuts, excavations, new construction, and sandy or gravelly beaches. Follow streams and rivers. Walk around reservoirs. If there are known deposits in the area, look in the grassy areas, ditches and in the underbrush. Examine all eroded areas with care. In dry periods look along receding shorelines and in swamps or bogs which may be drying up.

Careful study and determined examination of all possibilities will reward the patient and knowledgeable collector, but learn to be selective about what you take home, and learn to use the material you collect to best advantage.

Many hobbyists have pickups, campers, or vans for long field trips. Others prefer to use their cars and stay in motels or cabins or to camp out. While a passenger car is fine for most field trips close to the beaten path, most cars are not well-suited to long drives in the back country. Travelalls, Jeepsters, and other heavy vehicles often have 2 gas tanks which is handy

A club sponsored gem and mineral show or swap is one of the best ways to learn about the specimens in the area

for remote trips. In the winter a bag of sand in the back of the car is a safety measure. A first aid kit belongs in every vehicle. Some precautions are seasonal. Carry extra coolant in the summer, and in the winter have an extra blanket or two in the car. Always carry plenty of drinking water. When packing try to store heavy items over the axles as much as possible. Do not put heavy boxes of rocks in the trunk. Have maps and guide books in the front where they can be easily reached.

All field trips should be guided by basic safety rules. Other rules which will guide the trip are those laid down by the land owner or manager. Most accidents are preventable. Be careful and take your time.

Here are some time-tested safety rules:

1. Never work under overhanging rocks or on the edge of a crumbling cliff.
2. Don't go alone on trips to remote and rugged areas.
3. If your vehicle is disabled in a region you are not familiar with and you are far from towns or farms or main roads, it is best to stay with that vehicle. This is especially true in extreme weather.
4. Don't try to work out delicate specimens or find new locations if you are fatigued.
5. Don't stand close to a spot where someone else is working.
6. Don't go into old mine workings.
7. Be careful about walking on slippery rocks or crossing streams or swamps.

8. Never camp beside a flowing stream in a ravine, canyon, or gorge.
9. Do not drink untreated water from a stream no matter how clear it looks. Carry bottled water or water purifying tablets.
10. Light fires only in designated places.
11. Put out all fires entirely.
12. Keep picnic food cold.
13. Stay away from wild animals; they could be rabid.
14. Be familiar with the poisonous plants, snakes and insects of each area you visit.
15. Park your car where it is easy to see, and look for landmarks in each direction.

Equipment for a trip depends on the objective of the trip. If the destination is a mine dump to hunt for micromounts, a 10 power hand lens and some small tools like screwdrivers, awls, chisels, and pocket knife should be added to the standard prospector's pick. If the hunt is in a quarry for fossils which must be worked out of thick limestone layers, heavy mauls, crowbars, or mattocks should be included. For stream hunting, a gold pan and gem screens will add to the excitement. A long-handled tool is convenient for turning over rocks in gravel beds to see if a delightful pattern is lying face down.

Optional equipment also varies with the purpose of the trip. A hardness kit helps with field identification. A pump or spray can or bottle of water may help decide whether a piece of jasper or flint will be improved by polish. Epoxy, white glue, or shellac, soft brushes, bent wires, and burlap may be needed for fossils. Proper wrapping supplies are always needed. Other sensible supplies are matches, water, insect spray, whistles for signals, and a compass.

The long field trip should be planned with care. The most essential preparation is often neglected: that is, getting current information on the sites to be visited. Get this from clubs, dealers, guides, Chambers of Commerce, mining companies, fee areas, and Tourist Departments. Accurate maps are required. Write U.S. Department of Agriculture, Washington, D.C. 20250 for National Forest Service maps. For BLM maps and information write to the U.S. Bureau of Land Management, 7981 Eastern Avenue, Silver Springs, Maryland 20910.

Above all, any collector in the Midwest should always remember that access to the gem/mineral field for future generations may depend on the way he conducts himself. It has been a long hard struggle on the part of many hobbyists to find and keep open the sites we have now. Collecting is a privilege, not a right. Besides making every personal field trip a model of ethics and outdoor sportsmanship, collectors should pick up the litter of others as well as their own and report acts of vandalism.

Attend public meetings on land status. Write appropriate letters when the withdrawal of an area is threatened. Following the Golden Rule and the AFMS Code of Ethics, do everything possible to insure the future of field collecting.

Look along lakes and creeks throughout the Midwest for fossils and cutting materials

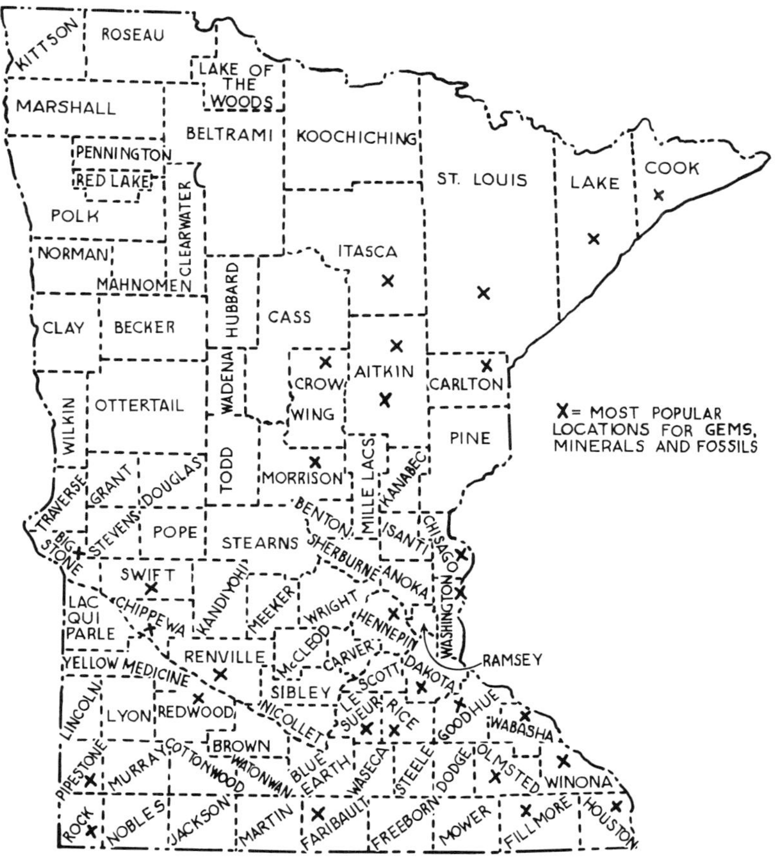

MINNESOTA

Minnesota's big contribution to Midwest gem collectors is the Lake Superior agate, its popular State Gem. Liberally distributed in the glacial gravels of the state of 10,000 lakes, its fabulous agates are still being found in many places. A rainbow of other cutting materials has come from the great iron ranges of upper Minnesota. The state is agricultural and industrial, and it also draws many tourists because of its forested recreation areas. Except for the north shore of Lake Superior and the iron ranges, most of the state is rolling prairie and flat lands. The Chippewa National Forest and the Superior National Forest cover large areas of the northcentral and northeast sections, and Voyageurs National Park is on the northern border. Fossils are exposed in quarries and along the rivers which flow into the Mississippi, which originates in the state. There are many scenic state parks, but most land is privately owned.

Northern Minnesota

An exceptional array of gems, minerals, and fossils has come from the iron ranges of northern Minnesota. The farthest north is the Vermillion Range, where the Soudan mine is the oldest and deepest mine in the state, and the high grade ore was 65% iron. Fine specimens of iron minerals and spectacular crystals of smoky quartz with bright inclusions, clear quartz with green chlorite, and red coated amethyst came from this mine.

Farther south and east, the Mesabi Range trends from southwest to northeast through Itasca and St. Louis Counties into Lake County.

Hibbing is about the center of this historic area. There was a time when the entire city had to be moved because of the vast quantities of ore on which it was located. The mammoth Hull Rust pit is the largest open pit iron mine. In

Iron ranges of Minnesota are noted for lapidary materials, mineral specimens and fossils

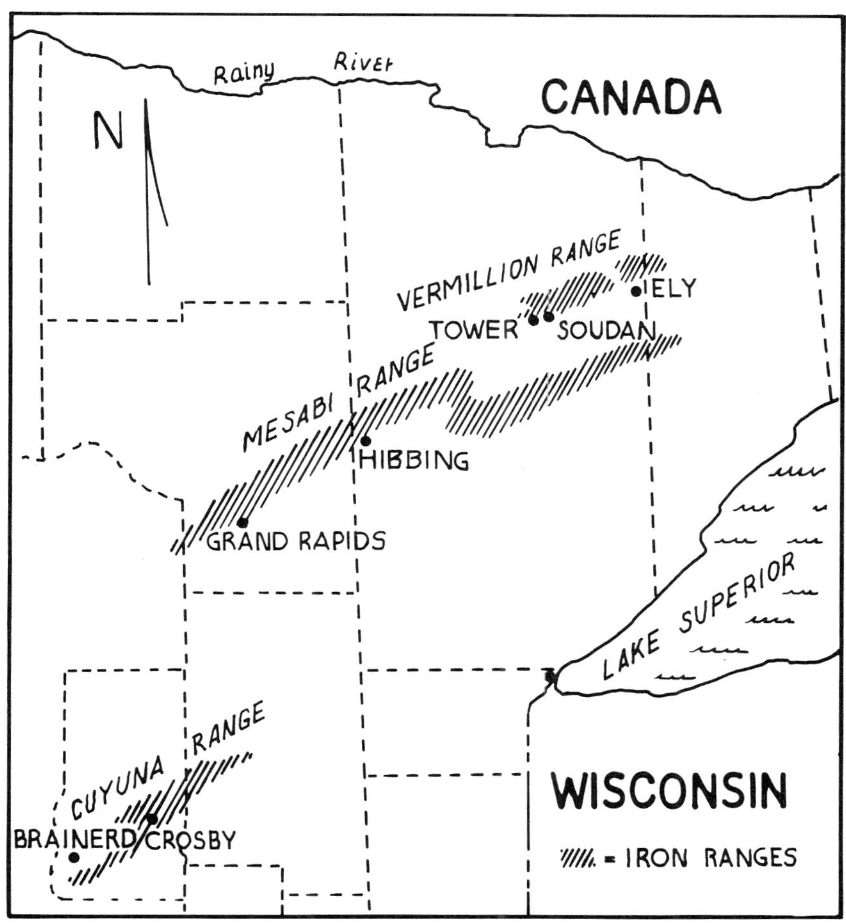

the many old dumps of the area there are agates, quartz, epidote, and polishable pieces of hematite or goethite.

The jaspers of the Mesabi are among the choice materials. One of the most desirable jaspers has been named "Mary Ellen", for the mine near Biwabik in which it was first found. A bright and lustrous red and steel blue jasper with graceful patterning, it can still be found in some old mines, although not in the original site. Stream beds, road cuts, ditches, and overgrown rock piles may yield some of this fine jasper.

Several variations and colors of jasper occur along with agates and other gem materials at Eveleth, Chisholm, Buhl, Mountain Iron, Coleraine, Gilbert, and Grand Rapids. The access route to this amazing mineralized area is U.S. 169. Some of the Algal jaspers are green, red, pink, maroon, and mahogany. Hematite is included in some of the quartz materials.

Exceptionally intriguing fossils of the Mesabi are shining heart-shaped bivalves replaced by dark hematite. Near Calumet in Itasca County abundant mollusks, arthropods, and sharks teeth are exposed. The headwaters of the Mississippi River are in Itasca Park.

The Cuyuna Iron Range is mostly in Crow Wing County, extending into Aitkin County. In 1936, near the town of Crosby, an amateur lapidary, William Bingham of the Minnesota Mineralogical Society, discovered a vibrantly colored quartz cutting material, which was named for him. Binghamite resembles tigereye, particularly the "tiger iron" now coming from Australia. Fibrous goethite, instead of asbestos, provides the chatoyancy in this superb gem material. Colors vary from gold to red to a metallic blue black. The rough material, resembling impure crystalline quartz, was abundant on the original

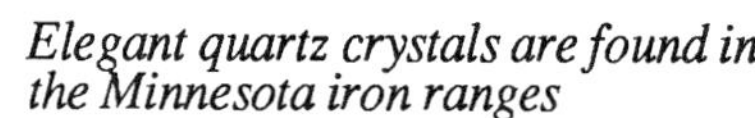

Elegant quartz crystals are found in the Minnesota iron ranges

One of the fine jewelry stones of the state is thomsonite from the north shore of Lake Superior

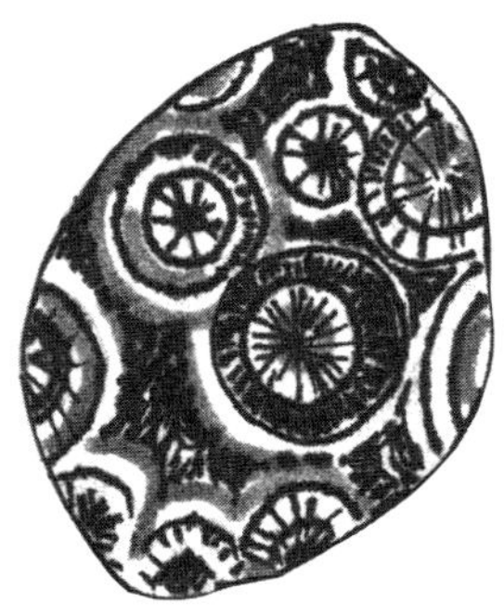

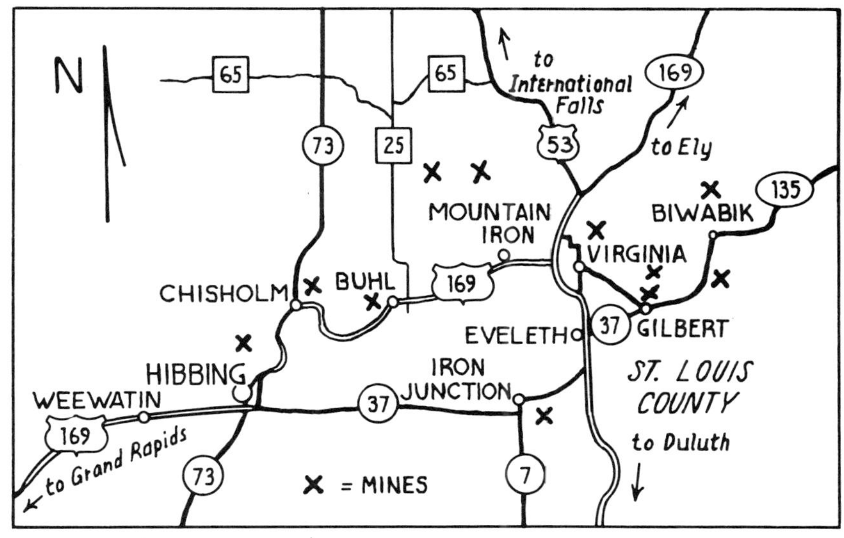

The Mesabi Iron Range

dump. Binghamite can be found at times in old dumps near Crosby and Ironton. The Arco, Portsmouth, and Hopkins Mines are said to yield some lucky finds.

Somewhat later, another Minnesota lapidary, Ray Lulling, discovered a material resembling binghamite, which he named "silkstone". The fibers of silkstone, instead of being straight and parallel, as in binghamite, are wavy and loosely organized. The colors are softer than binghamite, running to blues, greens, yellows, pinks, and grays. The dumps along Minnesota Highway 210, which are partially covered with dirt and vegetation, may contain huge chunks of rock which have veins of binghamite or silkstone. The long exposed rocks are covered with red dust, so careful chipping and washing are necessary to reveal possible lapidary qualities.

Agates are also found in the Cuyuna Range. Look along the roads, in ditches and excavations, in streams, around lakes, and in old rock piles. Look in gravel pits near Brainerd. With the banded and fortified Lake Superiors, there will be jaspers, silicified algae, carnelian, clear chalcedony, and other polishable material. Rhodochrosite has been found at the Hopkins Mine near Ironton. Nuggets of hematite from the iron range can be cabbed, faceted, or tumbled.

To study the beautiful gems and minerals of the Iron Ranges, see the Interpretive Center at Chisholm. Among the museum specimens are huge pieces of exotic quartz crystals, dazzling specular hematite, smooth botryoidal hematite, marcasite/ pyrite pseudomorphs, massive needle iron ore and vivid jaspers.

Psilomelane is one of the minerals of the iron ranges. It is a black manganese oxide occurring in botryoidal or stalactitic forms.

Grouthite was first found in a northern Minnesota iron mine. It is a hydrous

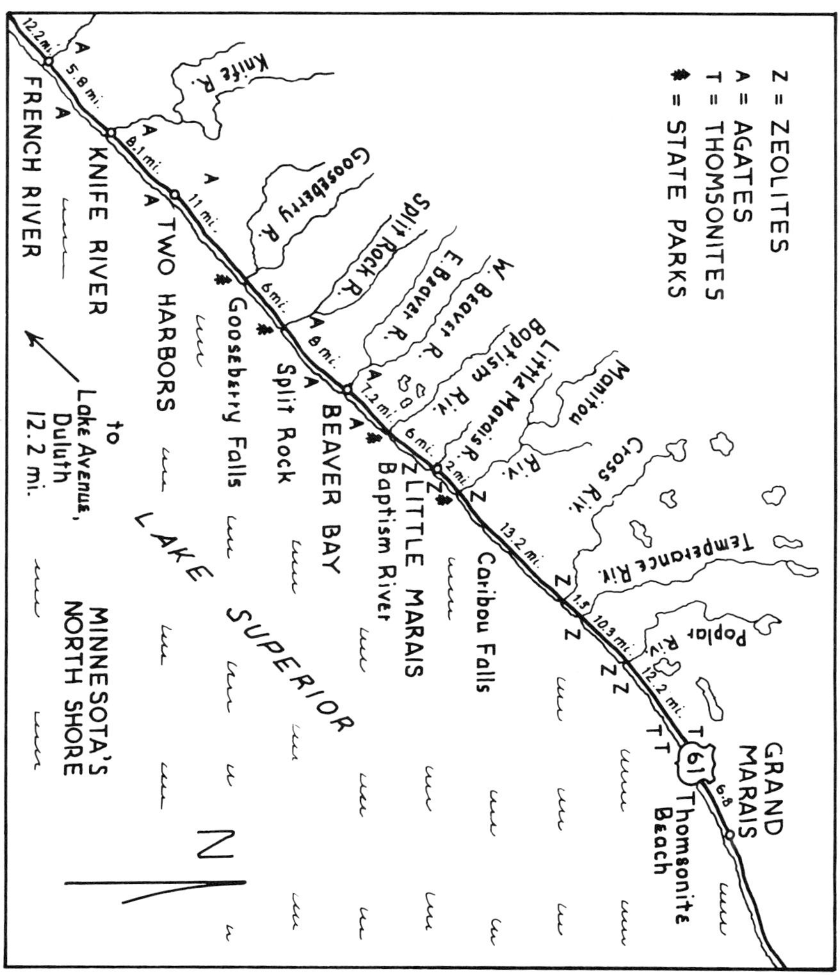

manganese oxide with a submetallic luster, crystallizing in small wedge shapes.

Ramsdellite is a rare mineral for the collector. It is a manganese dioxide, occurring in clusters of shiny black crystals in the Monroe Tener Mine at Chisholm in the Mesabi Range.

Manganite is found in black prismatic crystals in pockets and vugs in manganese ores. It alters to pyrolusite.

Pyrolusite is a steely gray mineral which forms needle-like crystals in iron mines. It also occurs as pseudomorphs after manganite and in concretionary forms and dendritic growths.

The best concentration of the manganese minerals is in the Cuyuna Range, although some are also found in Mesabi.

Siderite is an iron carbonate of the Mesabi. It occurs as a massive aggregate of very small crystals which are tan, buff, or brown in color.

Arsenopyrite is an iron sulfate which occurs in the Roberts Mine near Cuyuna.

All of the iron ranges have a diversity of hematite varieties. The best gem quality hematite comes from the Grand Rapids Mines of the Mesabi. Martite is a variety of hematite which sometimes occurs as pseudomorphs after magnetite.

Scenic Highway 61 follows Lake Superior's shoreline northeast of Duluth and passes outcrops of basalt with treasures of agates and zeolite. The agates can be found on the lake shore, in the river banks, and gravel bars near Split Rock, Beaver Bay, Two Harbors and French River. Zeolites are found in vugs and cavities in the dark basalt from Little Marais north to Grand Marais.

Thomsonites are the most sought after gem of the north shore. The classic locality for these dainty pastel zeolite gems is near Grand Marais. There are usually a couple of fee basis sites open to diggers. Ask at the Alley Agate Shop in Grand Marais. A motel near Thomsonite Beach at Lutsen, owned by the Fiegals, has collecting areas for guests. Thomsonites have weathered from the matrix in some places and can be found on the beaches. Digging along the edges of streams also reveals gems which have loosened from their resistant basalt matrix. Road cuts and high banks often yield pieces of the durable rock with small thomsonite embedded. Thomsonite hunting is permitted at Good Harbor Bay on public beaches.

Thomsonites are a little over 5 in hardness. Their structure is fibrous and radial, and their attractive patterns form bright concentric eyes. The colors are pink, rose, and green, with white and sometimes black. A translucent variety of solid green is called lintonite. Thomsonite nodules seldom exceed 1 inch in diameter. They take a high polish and make striking jewelry.

The rocks of upper Minnesota are mostly metasedimentary, such as graywacke interlayered with basalt, andesite, and pillow lavas. Basaltic flows outline the north shore of Lake Superior and there are large areas of igneous rocks as bedrock of the northern lake region. The iron ranges are metamorphic graywacke, siltstone, argillite, slate and quartz with deep beds of iron ore.

On the surface there are deposits of peat, loess, sands, gravels and deposits left by glacial lakes.

Zeolites are present in vugs and cavities in the basalts of the north shore. Some of these zeolites are hovlandite, stilbite pectolite, heulandite, laumontite, lintonite, thomsonite, and analcite. Zeolites are used as water softeners but are found here as delicate and esthetic crystals.

Basanite, or Lydian touchstone, is another of the northshore minerals. It has been found near Grand Marais. A fine-grained jaspery black quartz, it is used in the assay process.

Pistachio green epidote crystals are sometimes found on the north shore in cavities in the basalts and sometimes in rocks of the glacial drift.

Prehnite, sometimes flecked with bright native copper, is found at Good Harbor Bay. The prehnite is pale green and is found as water worn pebbles.

Ilmenite, an iron titanium oxide which lacks magnetism, is found in Lake and Cook Counties north and east of Duluth. Arsenopyrite, a silvery white mineral, is found in veins at the west end of Loon Lake in Cook County.

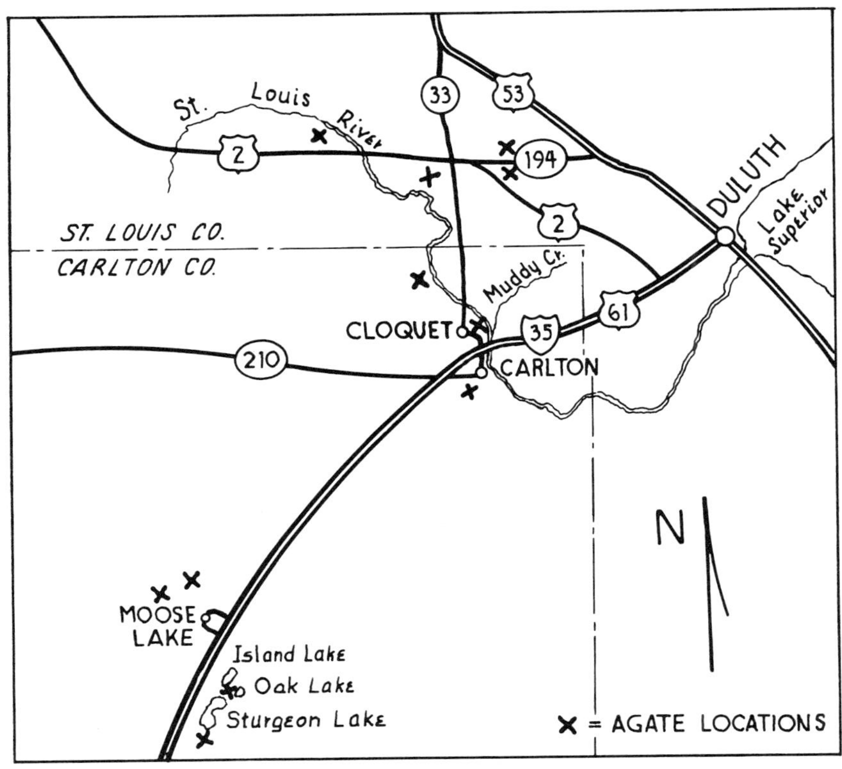

Lake Superior agate locations in Carlton and St. Louis Counties

In the basalt, 13 miles east of Grand Marais, is another of Minnesota's home grown agates, Paradise Beach agate. It is a banded agate with vibrant layers of white and red-orange. Another type of agate found on the north shore is thunderegg agate. The banded agates are concretionary nodules, unlike the thundereggs of the western states. They are found east of Grand Marais on a hill near the highway at Five Mile Rock.

Carlton County is probably the world headquarters for Lake Superior agates. The fact that the largest Lake Superior agate ever found, an incredible 108 pounds, was found only recently testifies to the fact that great finds are still possible. The late Jean Dahlberg, an authority on Minnesota gemstones, said that the second largest Lake Superior agate, weighing almost 50 pounds, also came from this county. Several agates weighing from 15 to 25 pounds have also come from Carlton County. Agates are found in gravel pits, ditches, along the railroad tracks and roadways, and along the rivers and lakes in all directions from Moose Lake. Moose Lake sponsors an annual "Agate Days" celebration to the delight of agate fanciers from all over the country.

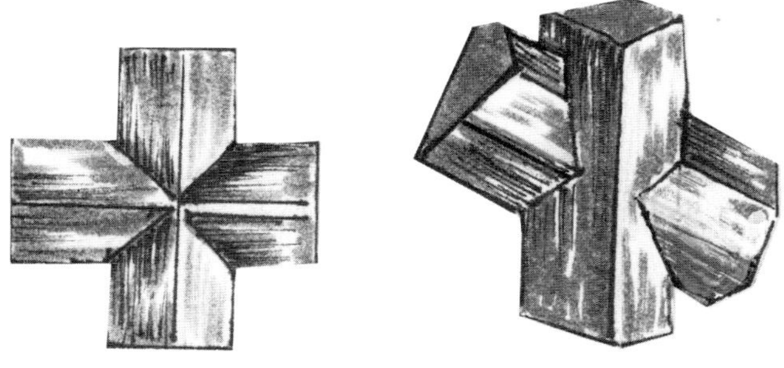

Two forms of staurolite crystals are from Royalton

Southern Minnesota

Staurolite crystals, commonly called "fairy crosses" are found near Little Falls and Royalton in Morrison County. The twinned crystals are found in schists along the Mississippi River near Little Falls and below the dam east of Royalton. Brown in color, the cruciform or "x" shaped twinned crystals and single crystals can be found in the schist matrix, or weathered out in the sands along the shore, or under bridges. Small garnet crystals are found in these same schists and sands.

Agates and other quartz gems are found in Big Stone, Swift, Chippewa, Renville and Redwood Counties in southeastern Minnesota. Renville County

Staurolite crystal locations near Royalton, Minnesota

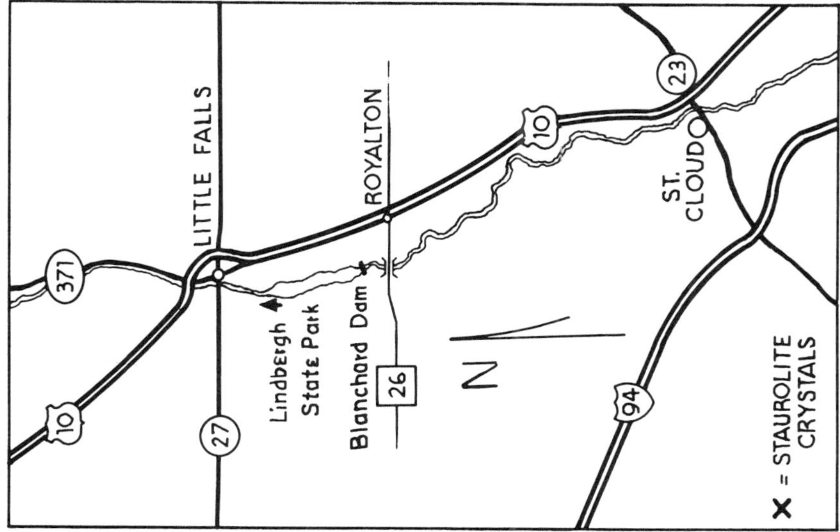

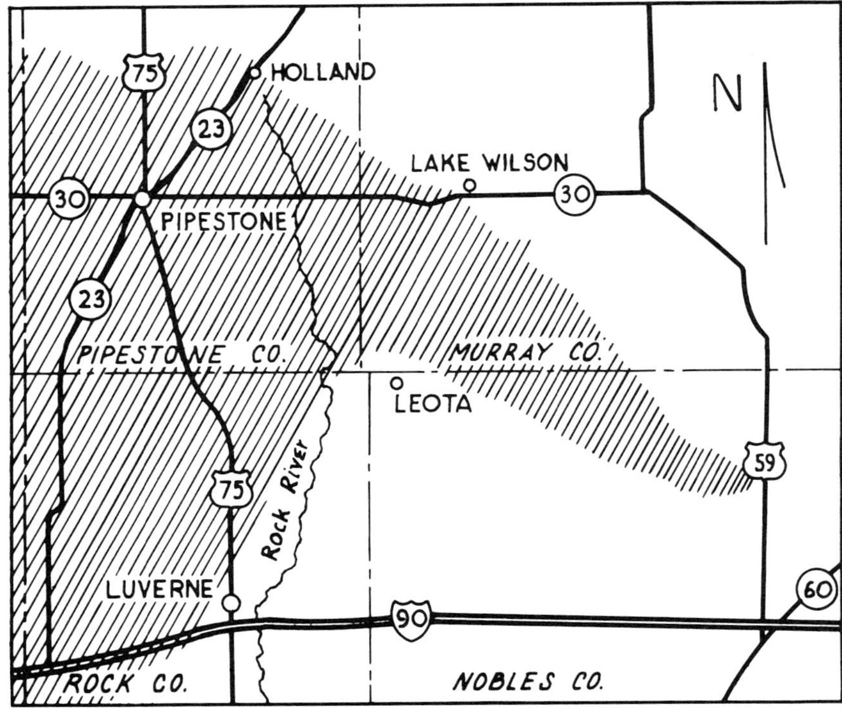

The shaded area shows the extent of catlinite and quartzite deposits in southwestern Minnesota

is also known to fossil collectors because of a fossiliferous layer which is exposed on the banks of Hawk Creek. Delicate leaf prints of the Cretaceous period are found in road cuts along county roads 19 and 12. The best exposure is at the intersection of these routes, on the southeast.

The type locality for the clay mineral catlinite or "pipestone" is at Pipestone National Monument in Pipestone County in southeastern Minnesota. No collecting is allowed here, except for Indian tribes, but the park is worth a visit for anyone interested in minerals, archeology, or history. The red catlinite is interbedded with the equally red Sioux quartzite, and both materials are found as float and in outcrops many miles from the National Monument. There are in-situ locations along some creeks. Small trilobites have also been found in Pipestone County. Not a gem material, pipestone is used for carvings and decorative items.

Agate locations of southcentral Minnesota are south and west of St. Cloud in Benton and Sherburne Counties and in Le Sueur and Blue Earth and Faribault Counties.

A high grade pinkish and yellowish dolomitic limestone is quarried at Kasota in Le Sueur County, south of St. Peter. Called Kasota stone, huge pieces of the polishable material are cut and polished for many ornamental purposes, such as decorations for banks, public buildings and churches.

Quarries in the St. Paul area expose sponges, corals, and bryzoans of the Ordovician Period. Gastropods, pelecypods and other fossils are abundant in the St. Peter sandstone in quarries and roadcuts of Dakota County. In Hennepin County, 2 miles below St. Anthony Falls, brachiopods, crinoids, bryzoans, cephalopods and trilobites are found. Some cutting material is also found in the Twin Cities area.

Fossil beds are exposed in Chisago and Washington Counties. Look in gullies and washes along the St. Croix River from Taylors Falls to Marine where the fossil exposures are in the lower parts of the creek beds. Trilobites are found here on tan limestone matrix. There is some public access at Curtain Falls and Taylors Falls.

Goodhue County has been a major agate collecting site. Gravel operations on the Mississippi River at Red Wing have yielded many select Lake Superior agates, plus numerous other cryptocrystalline quartzes and other cutting materials. If the quarries are closed, try hunting along the country roads. The bluffs at Red Wing also have trilobites. Look along the railroad track about a third of the way towards the top of the bluffs; float copper is occasionally found in the gravels here.

Rice County and Olmsted County both have agate locations and fossil locations. Good collecting has been along the Straight River and quarries in Rice County and 4 miles southeast of Rochester in Olmsted County.

Winona in Winona County is a prolific producer of Lake Superior agates and all of the colorful lapidary materials associated with the lakers in alluvial deposits. Quarries at Winona were closed because of MSHA regulations, but there have been some reports of sponsored groups with proper safety equipment and their own insurance being allowed to collect. Permission must be obtained.

In excavations near Winona, trilobites, brachiopods, and cephalopods occur. Above the foot of Observatory Bluff 1/2 mile, fossil shells are abundant in the St. Croix sandstone. There are many marine fossils in the shale at Dakota. Silurian fossils are found south of St. Charles, among them trilobites, brachiopods and cephalopods. Brachiopods occur in shale at Fremont.

Lake Superior agates are found in Wabash and Houston Counties. Copper nuggets have been reported from the gravels of Houston County. Fossiliferous limestone is found in Houston County and neighboring Fillmore County. Locations are along County Road 8 near Sugar Creek 1 1/2 miles west of Fountain and at the railroad underpass 3 1/2 miles southwest of Spring Grove on State 44. There are dolomitic bluffs north of Spring Valley with trilobites and bryzoans. Trilobites occur at Weisbachs Dam. Quarries at Forestville and Granger have mollusks, corals, and crinoids. Many fossils can be found 6.8 miles north of Fountain. Trilobites can be discovered in the limestone near Wykoff.

For gem collectors there is a good chance of finding Lake Superior agates in almost any part of the state, except the northwestern corner. There are many lakes and rivers and streams in the state which provide unusual opportunities to knowledgeable collectors. The agates have been found along country roads and in plowed fields. Farmers' rock piles and construction sites furnish more opportunities.

Lake Superior agates are highly prized for their bright colors, their fine banding, their translucency, and their variety. Some of the best agates have bold eye patterns; others have straight or onyx banding in brown and white, red and white, or gray or black and white.

The Lake Superior fortification agates are among the favorites. The fortification patterns are sharply indented and the individual bands tend to be somewhat wider than the agates with more regular and even bands. Unlike the fortification agates of Mexico or South Dakota which may have several distinct colors in one nodule, the Lake Superior fortification agates tend to be homogeneous. That is, they have one dominant color, usually some shade of red with neutrals such as whites or grays.

The most attractive Lakers have bright colors of reds, yellows, red-oranges, yellow-oranges, oranges, rusts, and bricks. Sometimes yellowish-white or bluish-gray tones are in contrasting bands. Some contrasting bands are translucent and colorless. The most common contrast in the showiest agates are bands of bright white.

Eye agates are almost always defined by sharp white circles in target-like patterns.

A few strange Lakers are called "shadow agates" and it is hard to define these elusive nodules. The extremely close parallel bands when held at a certain angle appear to have moving lines. This eerie optical effect is created by the number, depth and closeness of the fine monochromatic lines.

The Lake Superior agates do not occur with matrix as part of nodules as do some agates. Each nodule is all agate. In microscopic examination, the coloring of the agate bands consists of minute particles of iron oxide densely compacted where color is the most condensed.

A rare type of Lake Superior agate however has coloring which is strictly speaking not there. It is the illusion of all the colors of the rainbow in "iris agate". When the agate is quite translucent and has extraordinarily fine and close bands, and if it is cut thin and held to the light, the entire color spectrum can be seen.

Pipestone from Pipestone, Minnesota, was used for the peace pipes of the Sioux. This one is inlaid with lead and jasper

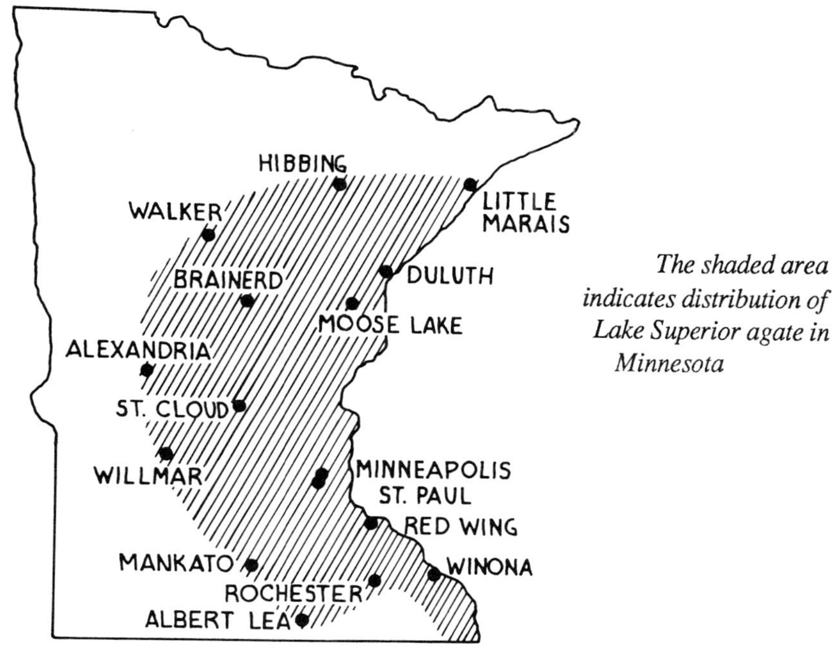

The shaded area indicates distribution of Lake Superior agate in Minnesota

On the exterior many of the Lake Superior nodules are irregular and "pockmarked". Some are well-rounded. Most exhibit thousands of tiny arc-shaped nicks and scratches, the results of many millennia of the natural grinding of water and gravel. Most agates exhibit some iron oxide staining on the surfaces which may be red, yellow or rust. These coatings may be lighter in color than the rest of the agate and most apparent in the pitted depressions on the surface. Although one looks for the banding when searching for the agates, the banding is not always immediately discernable at a distance. Look for color, a glossy or waxy luster, tiny pits, depressions and knobs, and especially translucency. If the stones are broken look for conchoidal fractures. A color more intense than the surrounding gravel may indicate an agate. Some agates appear to be bleached from long exposure. When cut they are much darker inside. Many agates show quartz areas on the surface. Bands or center patterns may be finely crystalline quartz.

The best way to hunt for Lake Superior agates is to walk slowly towards the sun. The sun's rays will reveal and accent the translucency so that the agates seem to glow, while the other stones remain dull and opaque.

At one time it was possible to sit on a gravel pile and sort out several pounds of select agates in a few hours. Now collectors have to work harder and be more persistent, but rewards are still to be found in Minnesota.

The Minnesota Geological Survey speculates that there are enormous mineral resources in the state, many of them still untapped. For example, there are 7 million acres of peat in the northern part of the state. Peat is a low sulfur fuel with a heat content equivalent to bituminous coal, and it can easily be gasified.

There are excellent clay deposits in the state, some of which have been used for pottery. Bauxite, an aluminum ore has been encountered in drill holes in west central Minnesota. In this same area chalcopyrite and bornite, copper-iron sulfides, occur.

High calcium limestone occurs in Mower, Olmsted, and Fillmore Counties. The red Sioux Quartzite from southeast Minnesota could be mined as a structural and decorative stone and for aggregate. There are places outside of Pipestone National Monument where the popular carving material could be mined. Traces of gold have been found in a few rivers.

Remaining iron resources are immense, and the manganese deposits of the Cuyuna Range are the largest in the contiguous 48 states. The present high cost of mining limits the production of both iron and manganese.

The basalts and gabbros of the Lake Superior area have commercial potential. Vanadium-ilmenite-, magnetite deposits, have been discovered in the northeast. Anorthsite, found near Duluth, is a potential source of aluminum. Clearly the mineral wealth of this state has merely scratched the surface.

Both Minneapolis and St. Paul have Science Museums. Minneapolis has a museum of Natural History at the University of Minnesota. Carleton College and St. Olaf's College in Northfield have museums with minerals and fossils. Another is at the college in St. Peter.

Pearls have been found in the mussels of Lake of the Woods, the upper Mississippi, the Rainy River, the Rapid and Caldwell Forks, and other clear swift streams of the Minnesota north woods.

The Minnesota Mineral Club is one of the oldest and most active in the Midwest, having hosted Federation shows several times. There are 18 other fine clubs scattered throughout the state.

Numerous dealers and manufacturers in the lapidary supply field are located in the Twin Cities and Rochester areas and in some of the many tourist spots.

Minnesota's State Gem, the Lake Superior agate, is found in most parts of the state

Pelecypods are found in quarries in southern Minnesota

Eye agates are a variety of Lake Superior agate

Counties with mineral and fossil locations in Wisconsin

WISCONSIN

The Canadian Shield covers the northern half of Wisconsin, but collecting is only in small scattered exposures. The glacial till is thick, and little bedrock is exposed. There is an excellent potential for mining copper, lead, zinc and other minerals in the state, but all at depths of 1,000 feet and more. There are numerous fossil locations in the southern part of the state in sandstone and dolomitic limestone. Lapidaries have found cuttable quartzite, granite, chalcedony, catlinite, moonstone, and Lake Superior agates, while mineral collectors have found stunning calcites, marcasites, galenas, and dolomites. With shorelines on both Lake Superior and Lake Michigan, and miles of Mississippi River border, the state's water resources are abundant. There are large. densely populated industrial areas, such as from Milwaukee to Chicago, but there are also remote forests as well as miles and miles of

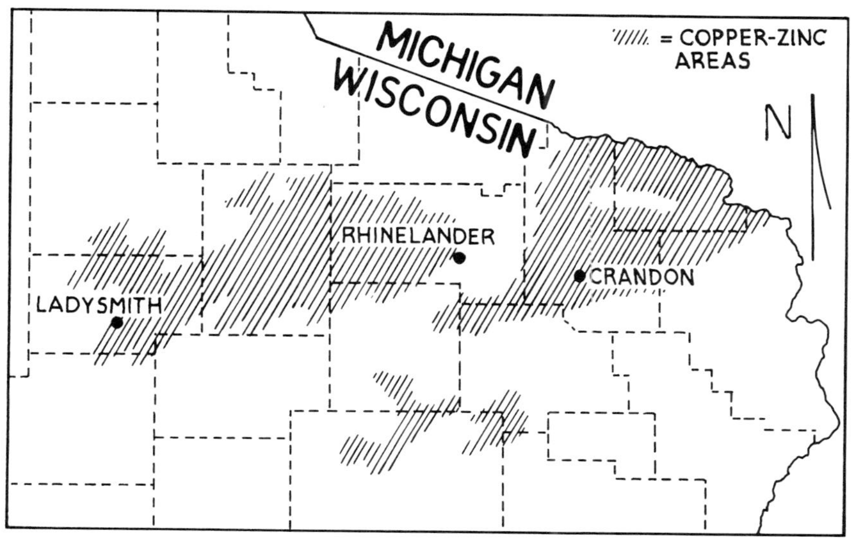

Recent copper-zinc discoveries in northern Wisconsin

farms, dairy lands, and orchards. Many of the older hunting localities are closed, but new ones have been found. Most of the land is privately owned. Chequamegon and Nicolet National Forests are in the northern part of the state.

Northern Wisconsin

Space age technology led to recent discoveries in northern Wisconsin of several significant mineral deposits. Several large corporations have been active in revitalized mineral exploration and are currently preparing to develop the most promising areas. Major ore bodies are in the Precambrian rock in Rusk, Oneida and Forest Counties. The Ladysmith copper deposit in Rusk County expects to start an open pit operation in the near future. Exxon has the Crandon zinc-copper deposit of Forest County, but is not ready at present to start the proposed underground mining. The Oneida County zinc-copper deposit was discovered by Noranda Exploration, Inc. and is in the Pelican River district.

There have been native copper prospects in northern Wisconsin in the past, and the band of copper sulfides is significant. Copper bearing ores were collected in the Ladysmith area as early as 1914. Light colored rock was found to contain lead, zinc, and silver in addition to copper. The Ladysmith deposit is also expected to produce small amounts of gold. It is thought that the Pelican Township deposit near Rhinelander will be capable of producing at least 1,000 tons of ore a day for about a dozen years. The zinc content here is important.

A cherty iron formation near Butternut in Ashland County also has copper mineralization. Core drills have revealed the copper-iron sulfide chalcopyrite.

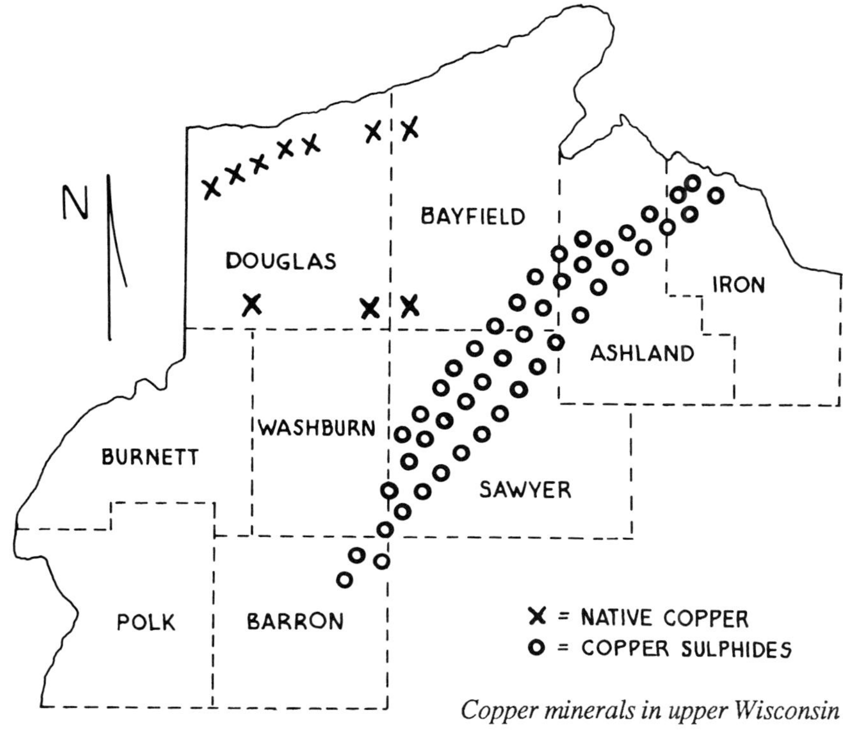

Copper minerals in upper Wisconsin

There are glacial end moraines and ground moraines in most of the northern Wisconsin counties. There are also large deposits of sand and gravel left by glacial lakes and the ancestral Great Lakes when these lakes were at much higher levels than now.

The iron deposits of Sawyer and Ashland Counties were worked in the past, and dumps near Hurley and Montreal yielded handsome cabinet specimens of botryoidal hematite and other iron minerals.

Dimension stone and crushed stone are products of the quarries of this large Precambrian area of upper Wisconsin where igneous and metamorphic rocks have been mined. Marble is quarried in Bayfield County on the Marengo River 25 miles south of Ashland. Some of the basalt quarried at Mellen, Ashland County, is porphyritic and makes an interesting ornamental and decorative stone. "Black granite" is the local name for the basalt quarried here.

Iron minerals, agate, jasper and native copper are a few of the collectables around the many lakes of Villas County. There has been considerable exploration for minerals in this part of Wisconsin over the past two decades. The targets are the rocks of the Canadian Shield which include lavas, basalts, conglomerates, shales and sandstones. Mineable ores are located at great depths. The chief obstacle to exploration has been the deep cover of glacial materials; some of the underground formations are enormously thick. There are few outcrops, but some of the best are the shale outcrops near Mellen on the Bad, Potato and Montreal Rivers.

A small quarry is located 1/2 mile northeast of Mellen on Highway 13. There is an interesting coarse grained gabbro here which takes a beautiful polish.

Vertebrate fossil remains have been found in the Pleistocene deposits of Vilas, Florence, Barron Counties and others. Other minerals which are present in northern Wisconsin, but are not being mined at present, are gold, silver, asbestos, kyanite, talc and feldspar. Among the potential resources of northern Wisconsin is diamond. Diamond bearing kimberlites were recently confirmed in upper Michigan by Dow Chemical Company, and the kimberlites probably extend into upper Wisconsin.

There are uranium concentrations in the granitic rocks in Waupaca and Shawano Counties and unconfirmed reports of uranium bearing quartz conglomerate near McCaslin Mountain. Mining companies have been exploring for uranium near the Florence-Marinette County border. There is thorium in Marathon County near Wausau.

A huge quartz deposit is in the rugged forested area called McCaslin Mountain where Marinette, Forest and Oconto Counties join. Quartz crystals and pieces have been found in scattered places over an area 4 miles by 20 miles. The best exposures are north of Townsend. The area, which is in Nicollet National Forest, is reached by local roads branching from Wisconsin

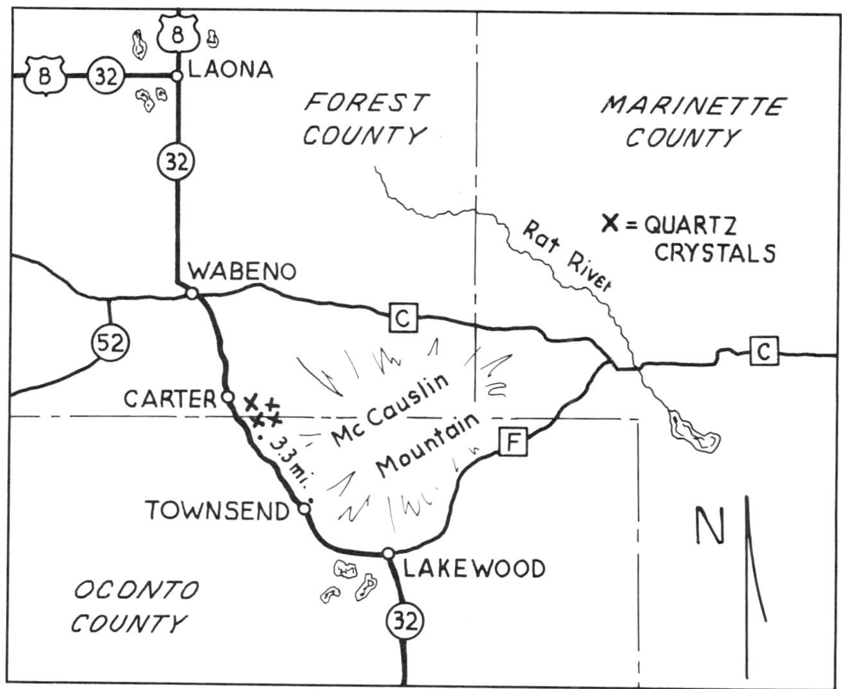

Highway 32 and County roads "C" and "F". One old trail can be found 3.3 miles north of Townsend.

The quartz crystals cover plates of crystalline quartz. Small and well formed, some are quite red due to the presence of iron. Specular hematite specimens have also come from McCaslin Mountain. Attractive specimens from McCaslin Mountain are seen in many Wisconsin collections.

Near Amsbur in Marinette County there are quarries for igneous and metamorphic rocks.

Lake Superior agates are found near Superior, Douglas County, on the beaches of Apostle Islands, and in gravels along the St. Croix River.

In Barron County, 5 miles east of the town of Rice Lake, catlinite or pipestone was once quarried by the Indians. In modern times it has been collected for carvings, and is now reported to be scarce. Also, in the Rice Lake area is some red banded quartzite which is quite attractive and similar to the Sioux quartzite of Dell Rapids, South Dakota.

Marathon County is perhaps the most interesting one in upper Wisconsin for lapidary hobbyists. Pegmatite dikes in the granites of the Wausau area have beautiful albite feldspar, known as "Wisconsin Moonstone" and "Wisconsin Labradorite." Highly chatoyant and pleasingly colored, much of the material is fractured, but carefully selected material makes lovely jewelry. The phenomenal feldspar is found near Rib Mountain and Marathon. Lloyd

The red granite of Wisconsin is a desirable ornamental stone

Brown reports an area for moonstone to be found in the ditches on both sides of the road on County Road "U" immediately east of its intersection with County "O".

Lloyd, who is Midwest Field Trip Chairman, warns prospectors not to stray onto the land of the property owner on the southeast corner. Wisconsin trespass laws are strictly enforced and most property in the state is private.

In addition to the moonstone of Marathon County there are quartz crystals, smoky quartz, zircon, fluorite, phenakite, garnet, chalcopyrite, cancrinite, gold and some rare minerals found in only one or two other places in the world. Many of these minerals are only of micromount size and are often overlooked. Al Falster, and expert in the minerals of the area has found large gold flakes by panning in local streams.

The best places to collect are the Wausau platon southwest of Wausau and the Stettin platon northwest of Wausau. Rib Mountain lies in the Wausau platon and has several collecting areas on its flanks and around its base. Falster collected a beautiful beryl crystal west of Wausau. Slate is found southeast of Wausau, schist at Athens, and granite at Granite Heights. Red granite, the State Mineral, is quarried at Marathon and Wausau. Several minerals are found northeast of Athens.

Nephrite, one of the two jades, has been found as float in Marathon County. The presence of jade had been rumored for many years. When in 1971, George Friedrich verified the jade and spotted large boulders in fields, fence rows and streams of the rural area near the Rib River. The nephrites occurs in a wide spectrum of colors, mostly muted or grayed tones or "earth colors." It is also quite opaque. However, it has been marketed to collectors and Wisconsin lapidaries and has been found to take a good polish.

Other minerals which have been found in northern Wisconsin quarries, excavations and road cuts are epidote, staurolite, apatite, barite, diopside, cordierite, magnetite and rutile.

Three counties in northwestern Wisconsin are popular for fossil collectors. In St. Croix County in the sandstone of the upper Cambrian Era, brachiopods, trilobites, and worm borings are found along Willow Creek near Hudson. In a quarry at Colfax, Dunn County, many species of fossils are exposed. At Mt. Washington, in Eau Claire County, abundant marine fossils are present in the quarries. Lake Superior agates and other cutting materials are found in river gravels.

Southern Wisconsin

In southern Wisconsin, there are brachiopods, trilobites and other fossils in the upper Cambrian sandstone in roadcuts north of Whitehall and in the bluff at Trempealeau, in Trempealeau County. Four miles east of St. Joseph in La Crosse County there are worm tubes and trilobites.

In addition to granite, there is an old iron mine at Black River Falls in Jackson County. The road to the mine is off Highway 54 (south), east of I-94 a short distance. The mine is closed, but taconite pellets and iron minerals can be found in road cuts, ditches and along the railroad. Attractive striped sandstone is present in Alma Center.

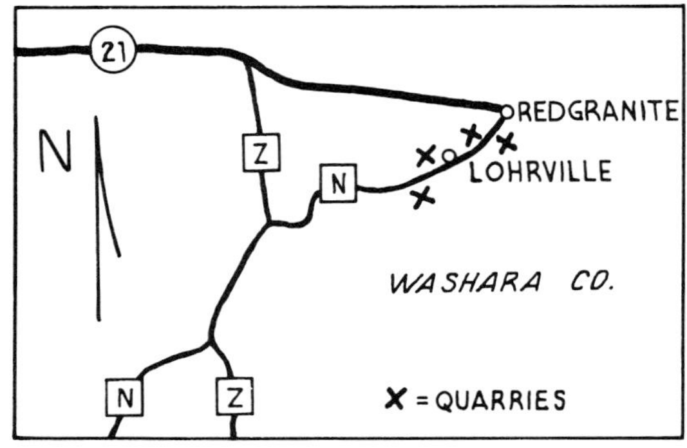

Quarries near Lohrville and Redgranite, Wisconsin

Talc is one of the minerals found in northeastern Wood County. Carvable "soapstone" occurs in a deposit near Milladore. A variety of igneous rocks are exposed near Nekoosa. Exposures are in quarries, road cuts, and along the Wisconsin River. There is a vein of rather colorful quartzite in Wood County, some of which is filled with small twinkling flakes of bright goethite or some other iron mineral and is classed as aventurine. Wisconsin lapidaries have had good results with this material. Granite occurs east of Marshfield, conglomerate and chert at Power Bluff, and peridotite west of Rudolph.

In the Waupaca area, Waupaca County, Rapakivi granite occurs. This is a distinctive red granite with inclusions of greenish chlorite between large rounded crystals of potassium feldspar rimmed with plagioclase feldspar. The showy material was once used as building and monument stone. The ornamental granite is north from Waupaca on Highway 49 to Elm Valley Road. Take Elm Valley Road to Granite Quarry Road. Turn right, east on Granite Quarry road 2 miles. Stop at the overgrown quarry on the left, opposite the Little Wolf River.

Waushara County quarries near Redgranite and Lohrville are for the vivid red granite which is Wisconsin's most admired dimension stone. Flynn's Quarry of Lohrville is south of Road 21 west of Redgranite. Granite is exposed by the park roadside, and a granite ledge runs southwest to granite quarries at Montello.

Brown County has Ordovician fossils, such as bryzoans, in the maquoketa shale north of Green Bay and southwest as far as the eastern shore of Lake Winnebago at Stockbridge. The Door County Peninsula has fossil corals of the Silurian Period in quarries, road cuts, stream banks, and along the lake. Carol Anderson of Green Bay suggests looking along fence rows and in stone piles, too. She says fossils are easier to find on Washington Island, including brachiopods, gastropods, pelecypods and corals. Niagara dolomite quarries are found near Reedsville and Valders in Manitowoc County. The Silurian stromatoporoids and tabulate corals make striking additions to a collection. A quarry at Rockwood has corals, calcite crystals and gypsum. Gypsum is also found near Francis Creek. Permission must be obtained to search in these locations.

In Winnebago County collecting has often been allowed at the Schultz

Quarry at Neenah near Lake Winnebago. The quarry is on Tullar Road north of its intersection with Highway 114 west of Route 41. Found in the dolomitic limestone and shale exposures are fossils, marcasite, and calcite. Only groups with proper safety equipment and advance arrangements are allowed.

A quarry which has had excellent cooperation with the amateur collector is the Utley Quarry near Green Lake in Green Lake County. This is a rhyolite quarry and should be of interest to the mineral collector. Lester Schwartz of Ripon is owner, and material from this historic quarry was once used for paving blocks. The quarry is on Utley Road, just south of Highway 44. From the junction of Route "A" (north) and Route 44, go 1/2 mile east and take the first right off 44, which is County "Q". Turn left on Utley Road after crossing a railroad track and a swampy area. The quarry is on the north side of the road. Carol Anderson, Wisconsin Midwest Director, writes that the Green Bay Club has been pleased with their finds here. Remember to get permission and follow the AFMS Code of Ethics.

Fossils are found in Fond Du Lac County near Oakfield. Some of the material is silicified land will polish. Resembling "cocquina" in places, the fossiliferous stone contains well preserved corals, bryzoans and brachiopods.

In Dodge County, the University of Wisconsin-Milwaukee Geology Department owns the oolitic hematite property near Iron Ridge. Mining rights are retained by the Oliver Mining Company. Travel straight north out of Iron Ridge (not Highway 67); after 1/2 mile turn left, west, at the intersection with

Utley Quarry near Green Lake

Ore Road. Stop at the base of the hill before the railroad track. The ditches along the road have many species of Ordovician fossils of the Maquoketa formation. Shortly to the north a fault displaced the Ordovician layer. Follow the dim trails north parallel to the railroad track several hundred feet and continue northeast along the trail about 150 yards. The oolitic hematite is exposed in the carbonate wall base behind fencing put there to keep people from entering the adits of the underground portion of the mine.

Sauk County is a notable area of southcentral Wisconsin. In the vicinity of scenic Wisconsin Dells, there are 3 major state parks where camping is available. They are Rocky Arbor at the Dells, Mirror Lake 15 miles south, and Devil's Lake 15 miles south. Wisconsin Dells on the Wisconsin River is a popular tourist area.

Quartz crystals are found in the Rock Springs-Ableman Narrows area in Sauk County. Drive north on Highway 136 a short distance to Van Hise Rock and park in the parking lot there. Walk back towards Rock Springs 100 yards to look for quartz crystal in the quartzite breccia of a large fault. Van Hise Rock and the area around Rock Springs is a major field trip destination for the geology students from colleges and universities throughout the Midwest.

South of Prairie du Chien in Crawford County, there are excellent exposures of dolomite in old quarries. In the dolomite are some crystals of calcite, dolomite and drusy quartz. There is also some oolitic chert.

Crystals have been found near the Mississippi River near Bagley in Grant County. Fossils occur in road cuts in the Grant County Dolomite. One location is near Dickeyville. Go 3 miles northeast of Dickeyville on U.S. 151 and turn

Sphalerite, marcasite, pyrite, galena and brachiopods south of Platteville, Wisconsin

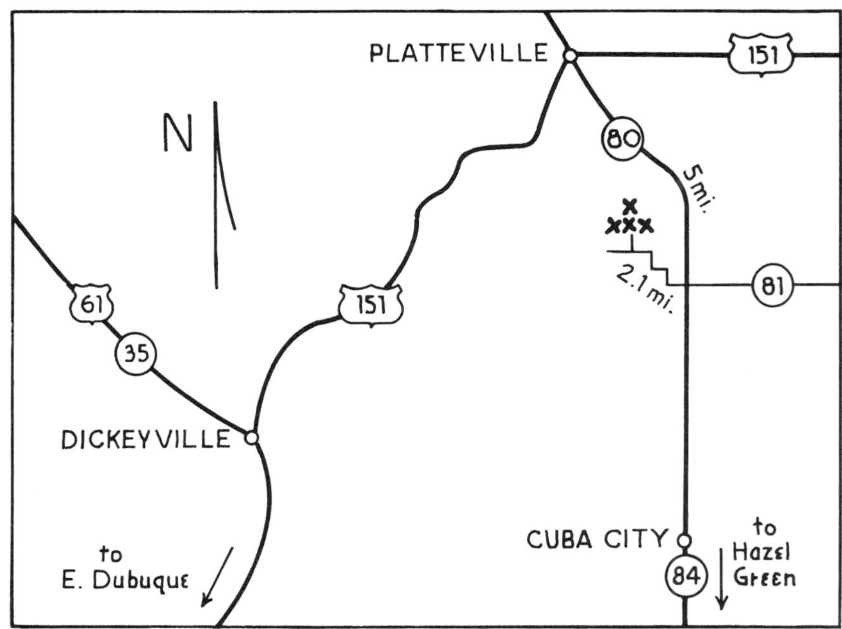

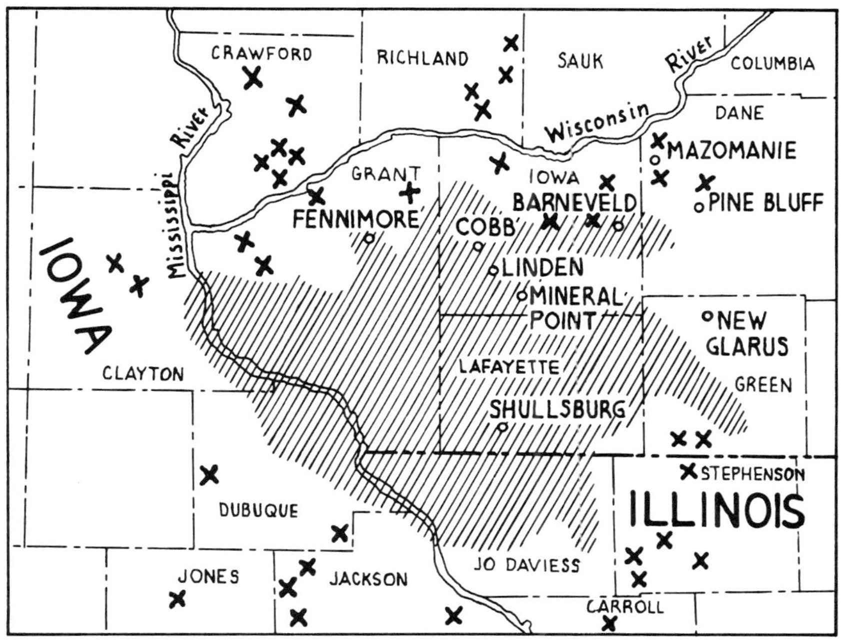

Shaded area shows principal mineralized area in upper Mississippi Valley zinc-lead district: the X's indicate mines

left, west, on Church Road for 0.3 mile. Keep to the left for 0.4 mile. Stop at the quarry on the left, where the road grade is steep. Look for bryzoans, crinoids, gastropods and other Ordovician fossils in the blue shale. Another location is 7 miles southwest of Platteville on U.S. 151.

The southwestern corner of Wisconsin has been an active zinc-lead producer in the past. The mineralization is in the galena dolomite of Grant, Iowa and Lafayette Counties. Some of the old dumps are accessible to collectors. Lloyd Brown recommends purchasing a New Diggings Quadrangle topographical map from the U.S. Geological Survey to locate the old mines and dumps. A few of the routes where old mine dumps are visible are Highway 11 west of Shullsburg, Highway "W" east and west of New Diggings, and Penny-Benton Road west of Shullsburg between Highway 11 and "W". Ask permission at the local farms. Turn the waste pile rocks over to discover sphalerite, galena, marcasite, calcite, pyrite, smithsonite and barite. Fossils are also found in some of these piles, among them cephalopods, crinoids, trilobites, brachiopods, bryzoans and gastropods. Fossils are abundant in road cuts on U.S. 18, 3 miles west of Fennimore, and in a road cut on U.S. 61, 3 miles south of Fennimore.

In Iowa County numerous dumps are five miles north of Cobb on Highway 80 and east of Mineral Point near State Highways 39 and 23. There are dumps near Linden on State 39. In Lafayette county, the dumps are southwest of Shullsburg.

Some of the other minerals to be found in the tri-county area are cuprite, chalcopyrite, malachite, azurite, aurichalcite, chrysocolla, marasite, pyrite, and galena.

There are good opportunities for fossil collecting in Dane and Green Counties. A spot for trilobites and gastropods is in a quarry 4 miles north of New Glarus on County "O". Also on Highway 69 north of New Glarus, there is a long road cut with many species in the upper half of the cut. Some crystals have also been found here. In Dane County, fossil algae is found at Ferry Bluff and Mazomanie. Corals are found 1 1/2 miles north of Pine Bluff.

A quarry in Iowa County 1/2 miles east of Barneveld on Cemetery Drive has fossils and crystals. At the intersection of Highways 23 and 130 there is a small abandoned quarry about 100 yards from the road with abundant gastropods, brachiopods, and corals.

Numerous quarries noted for fossils, dot the counties of southeastern Wisconsin. Some of these are at Cedarville, Grafton and Saukville in Ozaukee County. Quarries are near the Milwaukee River. In Milwaukee County the Hartung Quarry is a notable location for excellent trilobites. Sign a release at the Milwaukee land fill site. Brown says the trilobite strata will probably be covered over by 1990. Superb specimens from here are found in major museums.

Pyrite nodules and celestite crystals have been collected in the city of Milwaukee, where Janet Schitte collected pyrite in the hill behind the Dillon Motel and Hall Chevrolet. The celestite came to light when it was brought to the surface during the tunneling for the Metropolitan Sewer Project. Much of it was dumped opposite the Milwaukee County Stadium.

Lloyd Brown shares a favorite spot with fellow enthusiasts, Quarry Lake Park in Racine. Fine crinoids and trilobites are found in a reef bed here, and there are also bryzoans, gastropods and cephalopods of the Silurian Period.

More than 20 diamonds have been found in Wisconsin in the late 1800s, and in more recent times, some have been sought near Antigo. A diamond was found near Burlington in Racine County, another near Saukville in Ozaukee County, and one near Oregon in Dane County. Other diamonds have been found in Pierce County near Plumer, in Waukesha County at Sussex, and in Washington County at Kohlsville where the largest diamond, the Theresa, at 21.25 carats, was found. It has been speculated that diamonds were brought by the glacier. However, kimberlite was recently discovered in upper Michigan, and there is a possibility that remote parts of Wisconsin could have kimberlite covered by thick glacial till.

Freshwater pearls have been found in Wisconsin in Lafayette, Green, Grant, Crawford, Calumet, Manitowoc Counties and others. Wisconsin's potential as a mineral producer is great. Several companies are involved in exploration at present and have been for some time. They are secretive about results but are prolonging their investigations. There will undoubtedly be rich finds in the future.

There are two fine earth science museums in Milwaukee: one at the University and one at Milwaukee-Downer College. There are also museums at colleges in Watertown, Beloit and Appleton. Green Bay, Ripon and Oshkosh have museums as well.

Among the many fine clubs in Wisconsin is the Wisconsin Geological Society, organized in 1936, and a founder of the Midwest Federation in 1940. Several clubs consistently win Federation awards, and members are enthusiastic about conservation and keeping localities open. All visitors should help them.

Educational shows are at Milwaukee, Madison, Racine, Kenosha, Wisconsin Rapids, Eau Claire, and several other cities.

"Kidney ore", hematite, from the Carey Mine, Hurley, Wisconsin. Photo – Dr. Oliver Lohr

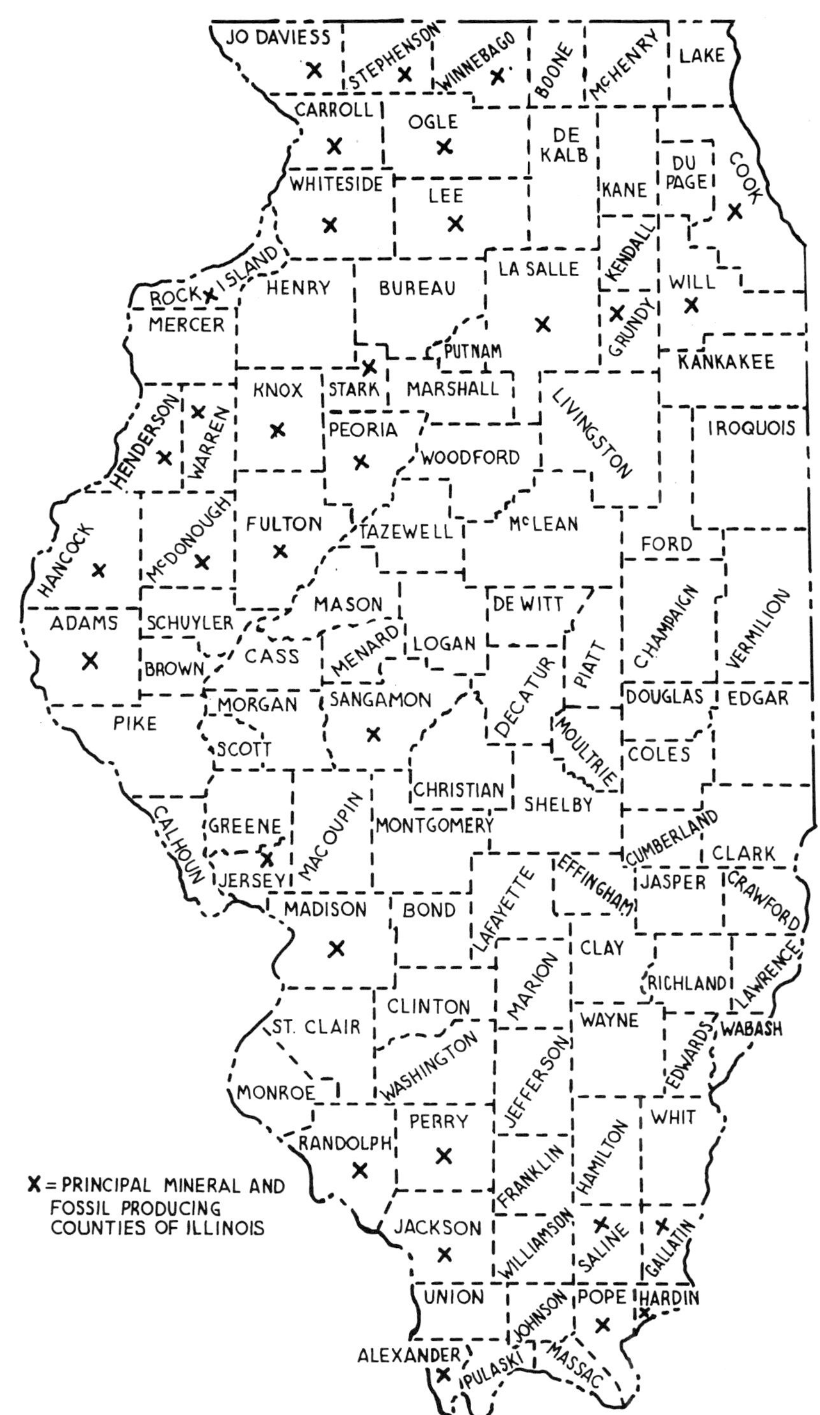
JO DAVIESS
STEPHENSON
WINNEBAGO
BOONE
McHENRY
LAKE
CARROLL
OGLE
DE KALB
DU PAGE
COOK
WHITESIDE
LEE
KANE
KENDALL
LA SALLE
WILL
ROCK ISLAND
HENRY
BUREAU
GRUNDY
MERCER
PUTNAM
KANKAKEE
KNOX
STARK
MARSHALL
LIVINGSTON
HENDERSON
WARREN
PEORIA
IROQUOIS
WOODFORD
McDONOUGH
FULTON
TAZEWELL
McLEAN
HANCOCK
FORD
MASON
DE WITT
ADAMS
SCHUYLER
CHAMPAIGN
VERMILION
CASS
MENARD
LOGAN
BROWN
PIATT
DECATUR
MORGAN
SANGAMON
DOUGLAS
EDGAR
PIKE
MOULTRIE
SCOTT
COLES
CHRISTIAN
SHELBY
CALHOUN
GREENE
MACOUPIN
MONTGOMERY
CUMBERLAND
CLARK
JERSEY
LAFAYETTE
EFFINGHAM
JASPER
CRAWFORD
MADISON
BOND
CLAY
MARION
RICHLAND
LAWRENCE
CLINTON
ST. CLAIR
WAYNE
WABASH
WASHINGTON
EDWARDS
JEFFERSON
MONROE
PERRY
WHIT
RANDOLPH
HAMILTON
FRANKLIN
X = PRINCIPAL MINERAL AND FOSSIL PRODUCING COUNTIES OF ILLINOIS
JACKSON
WILLIAMSON
SALINE
GALLATIN
UNION
JOHNSON
POPE
HARDIN
ALEXANDER
PULASKI
MASSAC

ILLINOIS

From the shores of Lake Michigan in the north, to the cypress swamps of the south, Illinois presents many faces to the collector. A large part of the state was glaciated. The state is bordered on the west by the Mississippi River, and on the south and a portion of the east by the Ohio, followed by the Wabash, and with the Illinois River transecting the state.

In the north there is a zinc-lead mining district to the west and one of the world's great fossil plant areas to the east. In the far south is the major fluorite district of the United States, an area where peridotite, the state's only igneous rock, outcrops. And in between, there are limestone quarries, gravel pits, and coal mines by the score.

Northern and Central Illinois

The historic old city of Galena, near the Mississippi River, in northwestern Illinois, is named for the lead ore of its once productive mines. The mining district of Jo Daviess County stretches across the state border into southern Wisconsin. Specimens of galena, sphalerite, calcite and dolomite have come from these mines. Other attractive crystals which were found here are anglesite, cerussite, chalcopyrite, limonite marcasite, and smithsonite.

Some of the galena cubes have been of exceptional size. One, used as a paperweight in President Grant's home in Galena, was over 6 inches in diameter and was covered with crystals of marcasite.

Resembling modern city buildings, blocks of Illinois fluorite are shown in many museums

Although the mines are all closed, there are active limestone quarries in the county. They are east of Galena, northwest of Hoover, west of Elizabeth, and also near Le Claire, Cordova, Menominee, and Pleasant Valley. Fossil corals are found at the north end of Terrapin Ridge near Elizabeth. Lake Superior agates have been found along the Mississippi at Galena, East Dubuque and Blanding.

There are many limestone quarries in Stephenson and Winnebago Counties. A fossil sponge, locally called "sunflower coral", is a popular treasure among the Ordovician fossils of these counties. Other "keepers" are trilobites, brachiopods, pelecypods and fucoids. Some of the quarries are in Cedarville, Freeport, Winslow, Orangeville and Loran in Stephenson County. The Winnebago County locations are north of Rockford at Rockton, southeast of Roscoe, which is also north of Rockford, and southeast of Morristown, south of Rockford.

Similar fossils are found in Carroll and Ogle Counties. Carroll County has excellent trilobites in shale exposures. There are also sand and gravel pits for Lake Superior agates and other lapidary materials at Savanna. Ogle County has abundant fossils along Pine Creek near Polo. Cephalopods are found in the blue limestone outcrops around Polo.

Besides sand and gravel along with limestone quarries, Whiteside County has peat deposits which are mined west of Morrison. Gravel operations near the river are at Fulton and Albany. Silurian corals are common in the limestone at Sterling.

Dixon is a good fossil location in Lee County. Corals, trilobites and brachiopods occur in the shaley limestone in the hills along the Rock River. In the quarries and road and railway cuts around Dixon there are many marine fossils. A quarry on the west edge of Dixon is sometimes open to collectors with proper safety equipment who sign waivers at the office. Some quarries are open only to supervised groups, and the collecting may be limited to Saturday.

Quarries containing fossils near Rockford

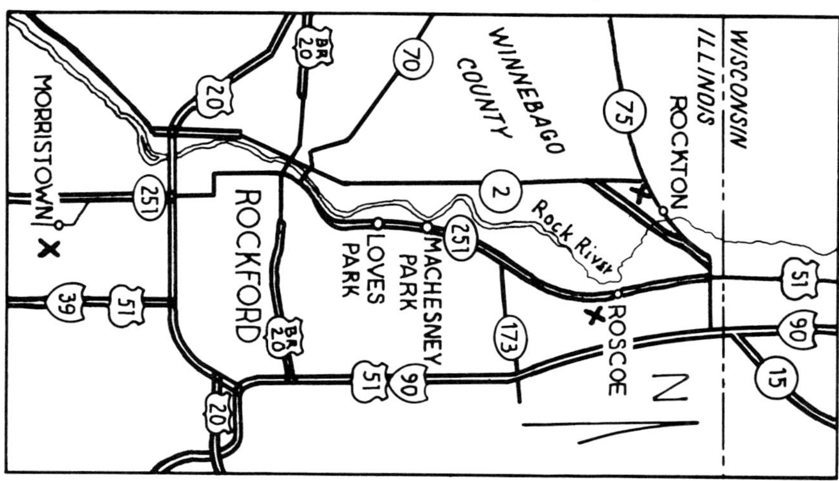

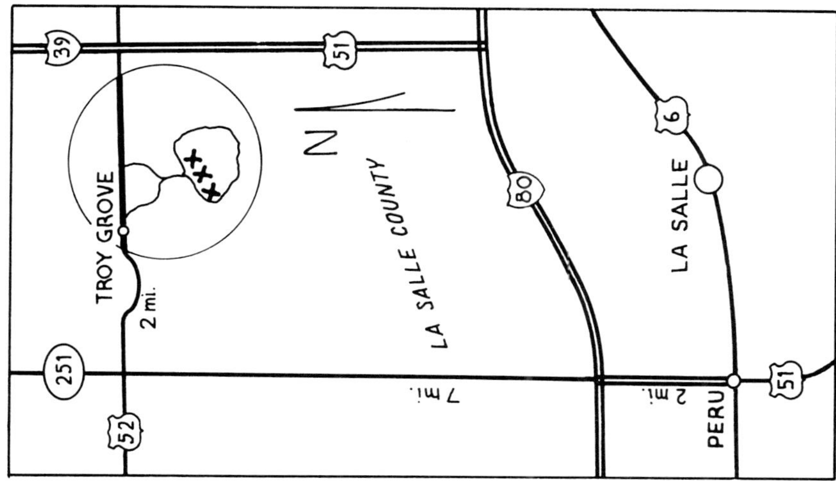

Location of fossils, calcite, pyrite and marcasite at the Troy Grove Quarry

A quarry in La Salle County at Troy Grove on Illinois 52 has calcite marcasite, and pyrite as a well as pelecypods and other marine fossils.

Devonian corals, brachiopods, gastropods, cephalopods, and more are found in Rock Island County. Outcrops are on the Mississippi and Rock Rivers and in Rock Island as well as near Hampton and Milan. Devonian fossils occur below Hampton 1 1/2 miles.

In Henderson County, Biggsville Quarry is 1 mile west of town. It is known for lapidary materials, minerals, and fossils. A similar quarry is at Dallas City. Both quarries are owned by the Cessford Construction Company, Highway 61, South Burlington, Iowa. Permission is required to enter these quarries.

A group of northcentral Illinois Counties, Warren, Knox, Stark, Peoria,

Location of the Raid Quarry near Biggsville, Illinois

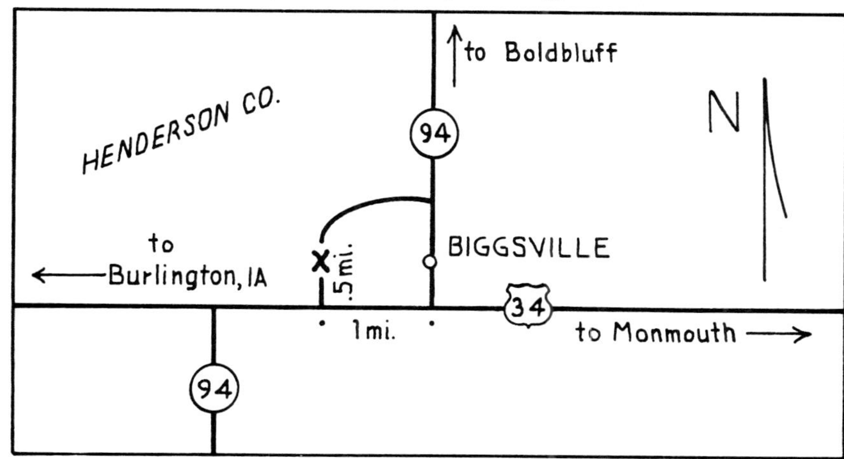

Fulton and McDonough is known mostly for fossils. There are coal mines and gravel pits in these counties. Exquisite plant fossils are choice finds here. Represented are ferns, cordaites, stigmaria, and lepidodendron. Some of the localities are Court Creek in East Galesburg, southeast of Victoria, the Edwards River northeast of Aledo, 3 miles southwest of Alexis, along Mill Creek, northeast of Pleasantview, Kerton Creek west and north of Bluff City, and Copperas Creek, west of Glasford near Colchester. Old mine dumps are the places to collect. There are many fossils in the old coal dumps and in limestone quarries of the Kickapoo Valley.

Interesting Counties along the Mississippi in western Illinois are Hancock and Adams. Hancock County is another of the Midwest's wonderful "Geodelands". Geodes with inclusions of crude oil are the incredible surprises near Niota. Geodes are also found near Nauvoo, Hamilton and Warsaw, and in the banks and stream beds of Crooked Creek, Brunces Creek and other streams in the county. With the geodes, in various limestone exposures are lots of fossils, beautiful crinoids, mollusks, corals, bryzoans and trilobites. Geodes are also found in many of the creeks and some of the road cuts in Adams County.

The amazing geodes of Illinois, like those of Iowa across the river and Missouri in the adjoining geode area, contain quartz crystals and numerous other attractive inclusions. High on the list of favorites are the "dew drop" geodes with small sparkling perfect quartz crystals frosting the quartz interior. Pyrite-lined geodes are glittering jewelboxes. Pink calcite crystals look like fanciful sculptures in a cave. Other inclusions are botryoidal chalcedony, goethite, limonite, dolomite, and sometimes galena, fluorite, or millerite.

Gray's Quarry at Hamilton was for years the foremost geode collecting spot in the region. Now it is closed, except for college classes with special permission. Other quarries of Hancock County are northeast of Warsaw (the

The tri-state "geode-land" of Iowa, Illinois and Missouri

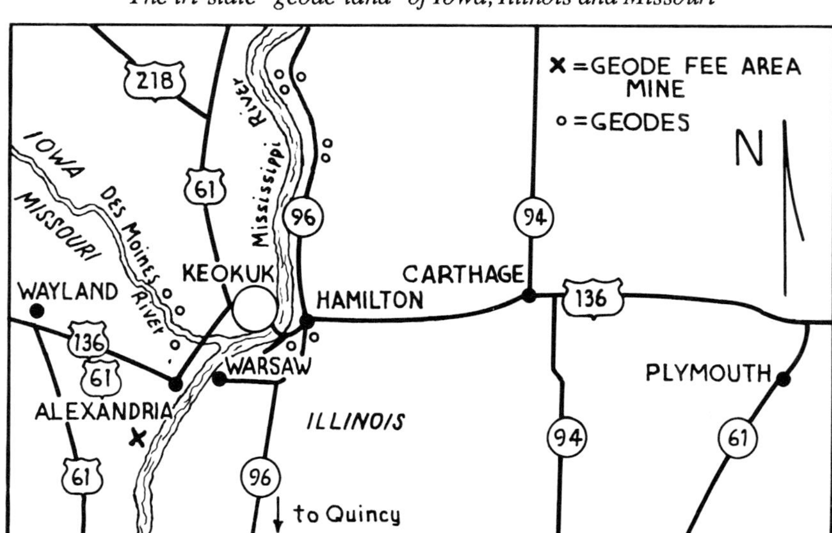

geode-bearing formation is named Warsaw), north of Plymouth, and northeast of Carthage. There is also a gravel pit northeast of Carthage. With the geodes are other cutting materials such as sunglow agate and pink colony corals.

Adams County has cutting materials of many quartz varieties along creeks, in road cuts, and in pastures, fields, and excavations. Geodes are exposed in a few locations. Look along the roads and streams near Payson, Liberty, Marblehead, and Carthage. Look for fossils in the coal seams exposed along McGee's Creek southeast of Clayton. Pennsylvanian fossils occur throughout the area in dark gray shales.

The Little Missouri Creek, southeast of Kellersville, near the Brown County line is a most interesting hunting area according to Hazel Kunz, an enthusiastic and accomplished hobbyist from Quincy. She says the coal shales exposed here reveal some fine corals and other fossils and also cutting materials. Permission is not needed to hunt in this creek. Since a road crosses it, direct entry into the creek is possible without trespassing on private land. Permission must be obtained before crossing any private land here or to hunt on private land in the county.

Illinois limestones were formed in the vast seas which covered this part of America millions of years ago. Illinois has the two principal varieties of limestone, limestone and dolomite. Limestone consists of microscopic crystalline particles of calcite. The calcite is derived from the calcium carbonate deposited by marine dwellers. Dolomitic limestone is composed of the mineral dolomite which is a calcium magnesium carbonate.

Some limestones were formed by the hardening of calcium-rich mud. Others resulted from the gradual compacting and cementing of the accumulations of ancient seas.

The dolomites were originally limestones, but magnesium from the sea water replaced some of the calcium. This rock became more porous and coarser in grain and texture.

Limestone and dolomite have many uses in industry. They are used for mortar, plaster, cement, crushed stone aggregate, agricultural fertilizers and mineral supplements, road building, ballast, construction material and more.

Most Illinois limestone and dolomite is quarried from open pits, but it has been mined underground along the Mississippi and in Chicago. The largest quarries are in Chicago, Joliet, Kankakee and East St. Louis, but there are other quarries in many of the Illinois Counties. The dolomite exposures are in the northern part of the state.

For hobbyists, limestone and dolomite quarries are major sources of crystals and fossils in Illinois. Occasionally some gem materials are also found in these quarries.

Northeastern Illinois for a long time was a paradise for fossil collectors. The fabulous "fern fossils" and other flora and fauna of the Pennsylvania Period which flourished here 200 million years ago were found beautifully preserved in concretions which were abundant in the spoil piles of the coal mines. Science museums throughout the world, as well as fine private collections, have prized specimens from this legendary era.

The Mazon Creek area, Grundy, and Will Counties are the classic areas.

Morris, Coal City, and Braidwood are three of the famous sites.

The remarkable fossil-bearing concretions were noted over 100 years ago, and intensive collecting ceased only a few years ago. When carefully split in half, the elongated oval ironstone concretions reveal fossils from ancient forests and seas.

It is possible to find Pennsylvanian fossils in northern Illinois outcrops, but the bonanza days of collecting are gone for several reasons. One area is the site of a nuclear power plant. Mining regulations require old dump sites to be covered over and replanted. Productive mines are no longer operating. The best chance now for collecting some of these intriguing fossils is a fee area at Dresden Lakes.

For a long time the Field Museum of Chicago was active in collecting in this area and in helping to keep sites open. Members of ESCONI, one of the country's finest gem, mineral and fossil clubs, not only made remarkable collections of the flora and fauna of the northern Illinois coal beds, but also published two books about these fossils, which have become a great aid to science.

Some of the old strip mines are now private recreation areas, and former spots of interest are now overgrown. The whole region is becoming industrialized. Although to tourists it may look more like a thriving area than it did long ago, it is a sad sight to the amateur and professional earth scientist who dreams of all the undiscovered species, now buried for good.

A gifted amateur named Tully split many concretions for fossil plants and animals. Among his unknowns were blobs which looked like lower invertebrates, and which looked curiously the same. Upon careful examination they were found to be a new species and were subsequently named the "Tully Monster" for their discoverer. The Tully is slated to become the State Fossil of Illinois.

Many other new species of plants and animals were found as well as superb examples of formerly identified species. Lepidodendron and Sigillaria, related to club mosses, are represented in the fossil concretions. Parts of leaves, branches and trunks have been found. Scouring rushes, related to the horsetails of today, have left whorls of leaves. Annularia Asterophyllites and Calamites belong to this group. Sphenophyllum stems, leaves and cones are delicate and graceful.

Both true ferns and seed ferns are found. Pectopteris, Asterotheca, and Ptychocarpus are true ferns and Alethopteris, Linopteris and Neuropteris are examples of seed ferns. Cordaites, forerunners of modern conifers, have left leaf and seed imprints. A remarkable reconstruction of important elements of the Pennsylvanian forest was a project of ESCONI and was shown at several regional conventions.

In addition to the leaves, stems, branches, barks, and seeds of long extinct plants, these concretions have illustrated animal life of the past. Some of the animals, in addition to the Tully Monster, are insects, crustaceans, worms, shrimp, salamanders as well as other amphibians and eurypterids. Other locations for Pennsylvanian fossils exist in northern Illinois, but many of these are not in concretions which have preserved the details to such perfection.

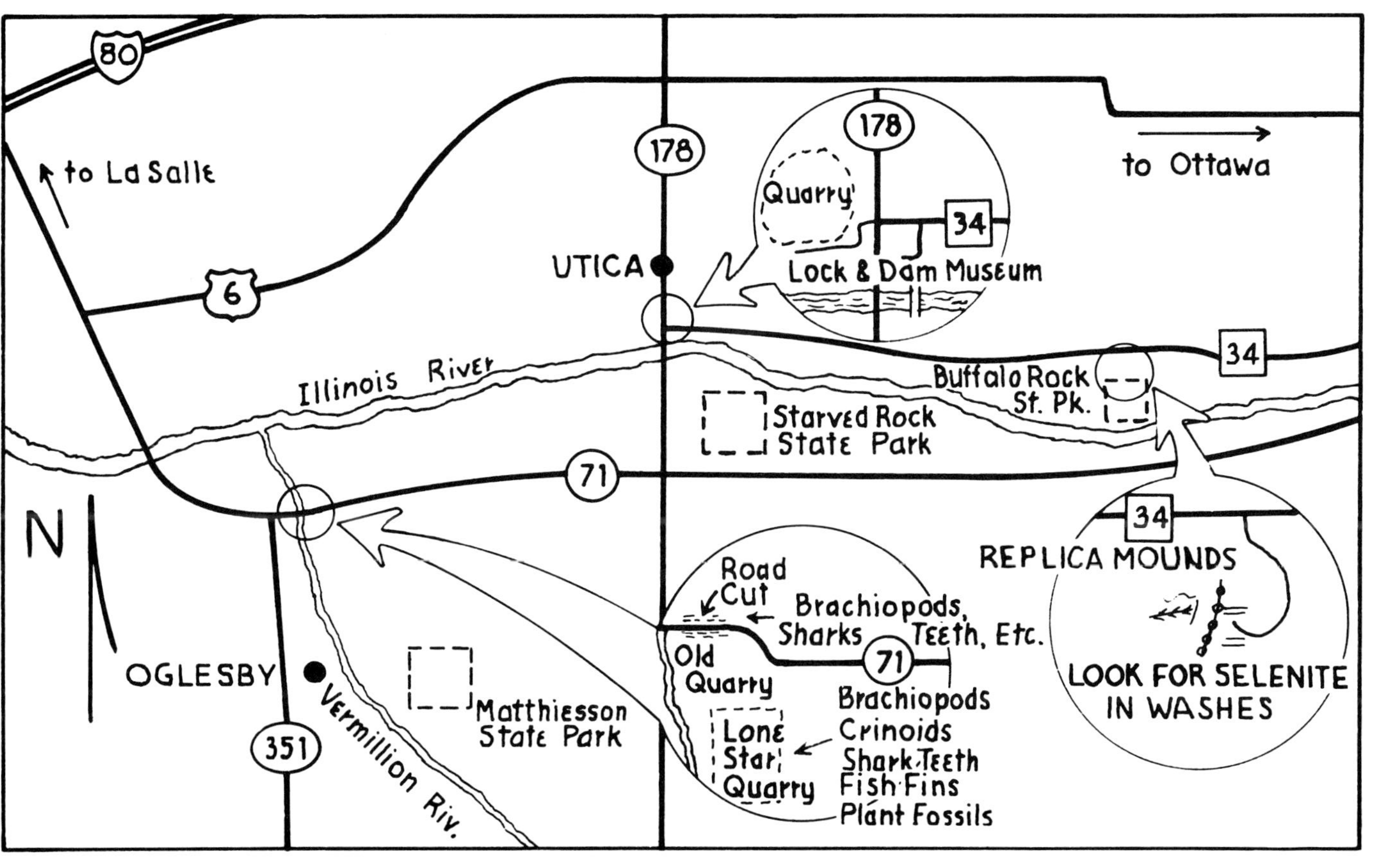
80
to La Salle
6
178
UTICA
Quarry
34
Lock & Dam Museum
to Ottawa
Illinois River
Buffalo Rock St. Pk.
Starved Rock State Park
71
N
OGLESBY
351
Vermillion Riv.
Matthiesson State Park
Road Cut
Brachiopods, Sharks
Teeth, Etc.
Old Quarry
Lone Star Quarry
Brachiopods
Crinoids
Shark Teeth
Fish Fins
Plant Fossils
REPLICA MOUNDS
LOOK FOR SELENITE IN WASHES

To split the fossil-bearing concretion, set it on edge with the long axis horizontal, on a large flat rock or other hard strong surface. Tap it firmly on the edge and it should break along the plane of weakness where the fossil is. Not all concretions have fossils, however.

Always wrap the fossils and label each according to locality. If pieces of the fossil break off while opening it, it is permissible to mend the fossil using white glue or waterproof cement. The fossils should not be coated with anything which might distort the appearance, unless the fossil is found to be extremely fragile. In this case, crude gum arabic in solution may be used.

Fossil plants and animals of the Pennsylvanian Period are found in La Salle County on the Vermilion and Little Vermilion Rivers. Quarries at Utica and Oglesby have fossil plants and invertebrates, and similar fossils are exposed in road cuts, and stream beds. Look in spoil banks of abandoned coal mines for concretions with fern fossils.

A quarry which has been cooperative with amateur scientists is the Lone Star Quarry off Illinois Highway 71 west of its junction with Illinois 178. There are abundant brachiopods and crinoids as well as some cephalopods, and in the black shale at the bottom, there are plant and fish fossils. Shark's teeth have been found there too. To hunt in this quarry, phone Mr. Johnson at the Lone Star office in Oglesby several days ahead.

Excellent fishtail twin crystals of selenite may still be found in the area west of Buffalo Rock. Buffalo Rock State Park is located 2 miles south and east of Utica. Access to the park is County Road 34. After entering the park, follow the road to the second parking area at the far west end. Park at the designated area and walk west through the fence to the Effigy Mound replicas. Look in the washes and bare spots for selenite.

The most impressive quarry in the state, or any state, is within the Chicago metropolitan area in Cook County. The gigantic Thornton quarry is south of Chicago and only a few miles from the Indiana border. Not only is it the largest commercial stone quarry in the world, but it has also provided a significant contribution to science. The quarry, an Eden for fossil collectors, has yielded a remarkable record of the 410 million year old coral reefs of the Silurian Period through the finds of paleontologists and amateurs. The Field Museum made an extensive study of these fossils and has an interpretive display. Among the many fossils of the Thornton are trilobites, cephalopods, brachiopods, cystoids, crinoids, and many species of corals.

The quarry is an active one. Its scope can be seen from the Tri-State Tollway which crosses it. The quarry is so vast that the huge machines look like plastic toys.

Scientists and hobbyists regret that this great quarry is no longer open to collecting.

Southern Illinois

In southern Illinois, there are limestone quarries and gravel pits in most of the counties bordering the Mississippi River. There are many coal mines in the southern Illinois Counties.

On Sugar Creek, 6 miles northwest of Springfield, there are brachiopods, mollusks and gastropods. Another Sangamon County location is near Virdon where there are several quarries.

A quarry at Grafton in Jersey County, has yielded excellent invertebrate marine fossils, among them ammonites and trilobites.

Geodes are found in Jersey County in several locations, but are most numerous near Elsah. There are many inclusions in the geodes. Some cutting material is found in the gravels of the county.

Agates. petrified wood, jasper, silicified corals, and other lapidary materials occur at Pontoon Beach, Madison County, in a gravel pit just east of town. Mississippian fossils are found 3 miles above Alton.

Randolph County is famous for its pyrite "suns" (which used to be called marcasite "dollars"). The flattened, round, shining, radiant suns are collected by the miners in coal seams near Sparta. The best chance to obtain one of these elegant collector's items is through a rock shop in Decatur, Blair's "The Pyrite Sun Dollar" or "Rusty's Rock Shop". The suns are available from about 1/2 inch in diameter to several inches. A new theory is that these glistening sunbursts could be fossil replacements.

Fossils are present in Randolph County quarries. Fossil plants and marine fossils are found in quarries and excavations near Chester and along Gravel Creek 4-5 miles north of Chester. Fossils occur in a bluff on the east side of the Okau River at Kaskaskia and 1 1/2 miles north of Prairie du Rocher.

Banded agates and other polishable cutting materials are found near Grand Tower in Jackson County. Also in Grand Tower, trilobites are found in Devil's Backbone Park. Exotic plant fossils are collected in the overburden of the coal mines at Murphysboro. The "fern fossil" concretions are in the spoil banks of old mines.

Another southern Illinois agate location is near Rock Springs Hollow on Orchard Creek south of Thebes in Alexander County. Banded agates, jasper and chalcedony are found in the gravels here and also at Tamms. Look for fossils along Orchard Creek and Clear Creek, on private land, with permission.

Mississippian fossils are found in the Millstone area near Robbs in Johnston County.

Fossils occur in limestone exposures in St. Clair County near Caseyville. Excellent fossils are found in coal dumps at Belleville and Pittsburgh. Look along Richmond Creek at Jack's Run 1/2 mile east of Urbana for abundant marine fossils.

There are fossil plants and marine invertebrates in the coal measures of Perry County. Dumps and quarries have yielded fine specimens.

Diamonds have been found in Illinois near Macomb in McDonough County and in Jefferson County. Pearls have been taken from freshwater mussels from streams of the following Illinois Counties: Woodford, Tazewell, McLean. Other pearls have been found in the Wabash River where it is an Illinois boundary.

Fluorite of fluorspar is an essential mineral. It is used in the production of steel, aluminum, ceramics, glazes and refrigerants. It is used in the smelting of metal, in aerosols, in toothpaste, in the manufacture of colored glass, for dental cements and optical lenses, in rocket fuel, in enamel and in

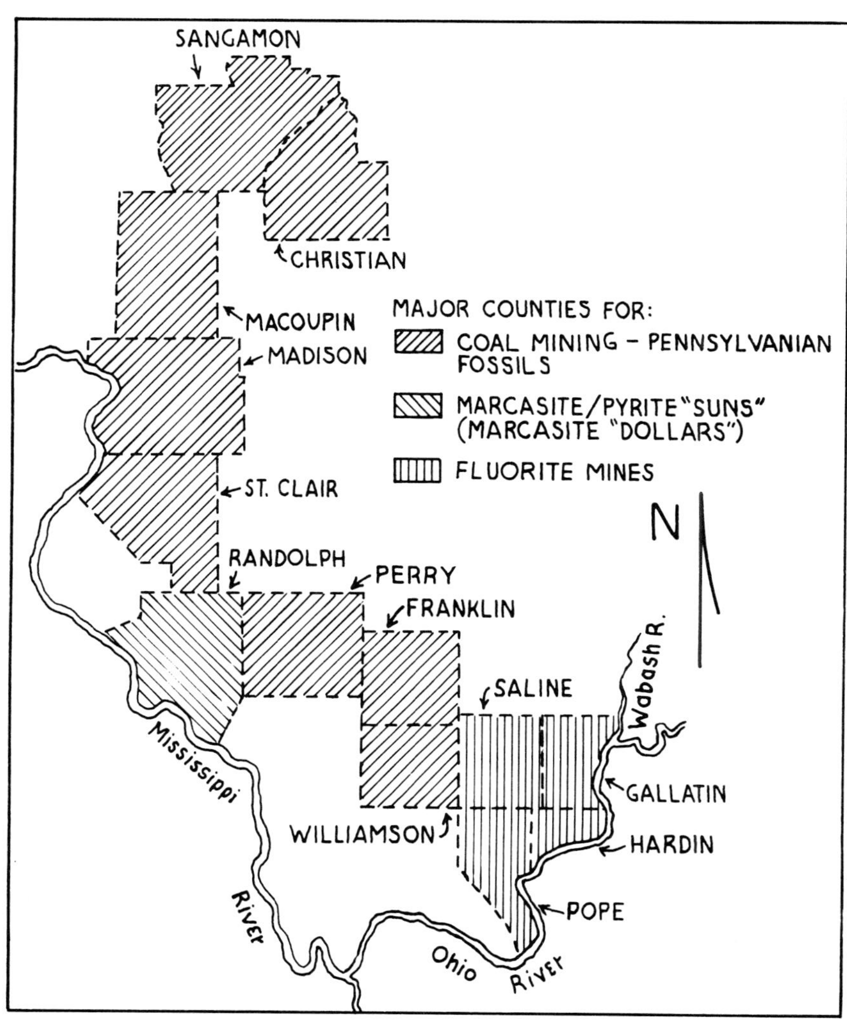

Major coal mining, marcasite/pyrite and fluorite counties of southern Illinois

insecticides. Great quantities of fluorite have been produced in southern Illinois, our nation's most important deposit.

The mining started in 1870 with pieces of fluorspar worked by Indians hundreds of years ago having been found. Magnificent colorful crystal groups are shown with pride in major museums and private collections everywhere.

The official State Mineral of Illinois, the fluorite occurs in glistening cubes in tints of violet, honey, amber, yellow, blue, ecru, colorless and green. The lustrous transparent crystals are color zoned and often contain phantoms and inclusions such as sparkling crystals of pyrite, marcasite or chalcopyrite.

Other minerals from the district are calcite, quartz, pyrite, sphalerite,

One of the many Bryzoans of the Midwest is Lyropora

Pyrite "suns" of Randolph County are dazzling novelties for collectors of mineral specimens

galena, cerrusite, siderite, anglesite, witherite, barite, galena, and strontianite. Specimens which combine combinations of crystals of these minerals with fluorite crystals are magnificent. For example, in Pope County large bright yellow barite crystals were found with cubes of purple fluorite, a dramatic combination. Spectacular specimens from Cave-in-Rock are called honeycomb calcite.

The fluorspar district is comprised of four counties in Illinois: Gallatin, Saline, Hardin and Pope. It also extends across the Ohio River into Kentucky. Pioneers in the area found the fluorite a convenient carving material and many of these unique folk carvings can still be seen in collections in Illinois and elsewhere. Miners also cleave the clear and brightly colored material into octahedra for attractive costume jewelry, for paper weights, and other decorative items. The octahedra are also popular for mineral collection boxes for school children.

Most of the mines were closed down in the recent past because of the economic problems which have plagued the mining industry. It has been cheaper to import fluorite from Mexico and other foreign countries than to produce it in the United States. However, some of the mines have now reopened and some production has continued. Fine specimens can still be purchased in the area and at shows throughout the Midwest.

Some of the clusters of fluorite crystals have weighed several hundred pounds and have been several feet across. Single crystals may be as small as 1/2 inch or up to several inches in diameter. Some of the crystals are complex and twinned. Forms such as octahedral, dodecahedral, and tetrahexahedral are intricate and fascinating.

The Illinois district accounts for 90% of the fluorite production in the United States. In 1981, 115,000 tons were produced, and this amount has decreased slightly year by year. The district covers over 700 square miles.

Geologists say that fluorite is a result of the chemical interaction of hydrothermal fluids which penetrated the Mississippian limestone of the area about 100 million years ago. The super hot fluids contained a rich variety of elements including fluorine and were driven up from a large underground body of magma by high pressure gases. The fluids acquired calcium from the limestone which, combined with the fluorine, was precipitated as fluorite. Although this process took place within the earth, erosion during the following eras finally exposed the fluorite-bearing limestone near the surface.

The mines near Cave-in-Rock, owned by the Ozark Mahoney Mining Company are active. Other productive mines have been near Rosiclare, Elizabethtown, Shelterville, and Eichorn. A stop at the fluorite museum in Rosiclare is a treat. Showy specimens can be seen in banks, libraries, cafes and private homes in the district.

Fluorite and associated minerals are the main magnet for collectors in southern Illinois, but the fossils of these counties should not be overlooked. Silicified corals come from quarries and outcrops in Hardin County.

Numerous invertebrate fossils occur along Lusk Creek in Pope County. Pennsylvanian gastropods, pelecypods and other invertebrates are found along the Saline River in Gallatin County.

Saline County has more recorded plant fossil localities than any other southern Illinois county. Try the area south of Harrisburg or the mine dumps northwest of Eddyville along with the south tributary of the East Branch Cedar Creek 6 1/2 miles south of Stonefort.

In Gallatin County the fossil plants are in a thick Pennsylvanian sandstone which outcrops in road and railroad cuts and stream banks.

Illinois ranks high as a mineral producer, primarily for its large deposits of coal and oil. Out of the 102 counties, 99 report some type of mineral activity.

In addition to the fossil fuels, Illinois has significant fluorite, clay, limestone and dolomite, sand, gravel, zinc and lead, marble and sandstone.

The clay deposits of Illinois are useful for ceramics, pottery, fire-clay, and fuller's earth. Industrial plaster and refractory brick are made from this clay. The finest quality, kaolin, is used for china and porcelain. Fuller's earth is used as a sweeping compound and for animal litter.

The best grade of Illinois sand is silica sand, which is produced from sandstone bedrock. Silica sand is widely used in making glass and also enamels, glazes, paint fillers, and for sand blasting. It is mined in La Salle and Ogle Counties.

Tripoli or amorphous silica is mined in Alexander County in southern Illinois. Tripoli is ground into a fine powder and is used for polishing optical lenses, as paint filler, and as an abrasive. However, to lapidary hobbyists, it is useful in many ways in the lapidary shop.

Fluorspar, lead and zinc are the other Illinois resources of note. There are peat deposits in the northern part of the state which are potentially useful as fuel.

With its extensive glaciation, its miles of great rivers, its Lake Michigan shoreline, and its many mineral deposits, Illinois is certain to remain important in this industry.

There are some fine earth science collections in museums in Illinois, some of which are in the Field Museum in Chicago, the Lizzadro Museum at Elmhurst, the Funk Museum at Illinois State, and museums in colleges or universities at Abingdon, Carlinville, Carthage, Decatur, Elgin, Evanston, Galesburg, Lake Forest, Rock Island, Naperville, and Sterling.

The Lizzadro Museum of Lapidary Arts is the only museum of its kind in the United States. Founded by Joseph Lizzadro, who was an enthusiastic gem hobbyist and collector, the museum has fossils and crystals as well as an exceptional exhibit of lapidary specialties from around the world.

Also important to amateurs is the Funk Museum at Illinois State. Lafayette Funk, a dedicated amateur, accumulated a large collection of impressive crystal specimens and donated it to the University near his home.

Illinois has many outstanding clubs, with the Earth Science Club of Northern Illinois being a national leader in educational achievements. Several clubs in the Chicago area unite to produce an excellent annual show, the Chicagoland Gem and Mineral Show.

Since the state has so far been friendly to collectors, it is essential that gem, mineral and fossil hunters always get permission and do everything possible to keep collecting sites open.

There are well-known manufacturers and rock shops in many Illinois cities, particularly in the Chicago area. Some are also located in Peoria, Rock Island, Rockford, Tonica, Springfield, Decatur, and Cave-in-Rock.

Trilobite, Kankakee, Illinois

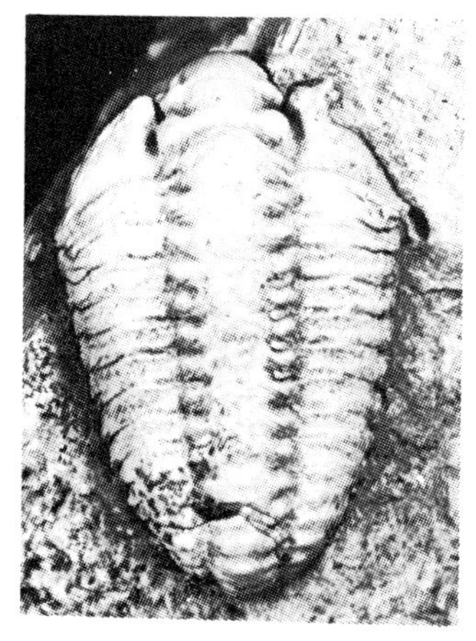

Pyritized snails, Farrington, Illinois

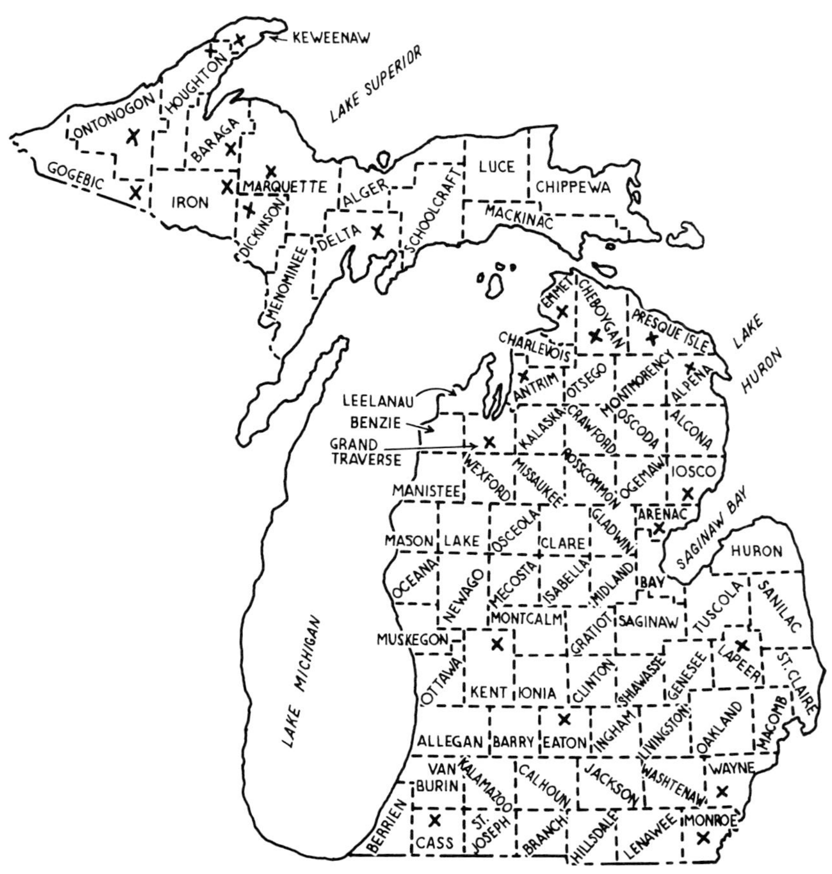

Michigan counties for locating gems, minerals and fossils

MICHIGAN

Michigan has a lot more than Petoskey stones! There is the amazing and historic copper country of the Upper Peninsula, worked by early man at least 3,000 years B.C. There are the iron ranges of the north country. Dow Chemical has recently confirmed the presence of diamond in kimberlites. There are agate beaches on Lake Superior.

The two distinct parts of Michigan are separated by Lake Michigan and Lake Huron, two of the world's largest fresh water lakes. In the Lower Peninsula, there are many gravel pits and stone quarries. Even the cities contribute to the mineral wealth of the state with an immense salt mine at Detroit and a gypsum mine in Grand Rapids. Natural resources and water transportation have helped make Michigan an industrial state, but it also has large forested areas and extensive areas of orchards, pastures, and farms. The Hiawatha and Ottawa National Forests are in the north and the Huron and Manistee National Forests in the south.

Upper Michigan

The minerals of the copper country are legendary. The cool, beautiful Keweenaw country lures collectors from all over the nation to search the

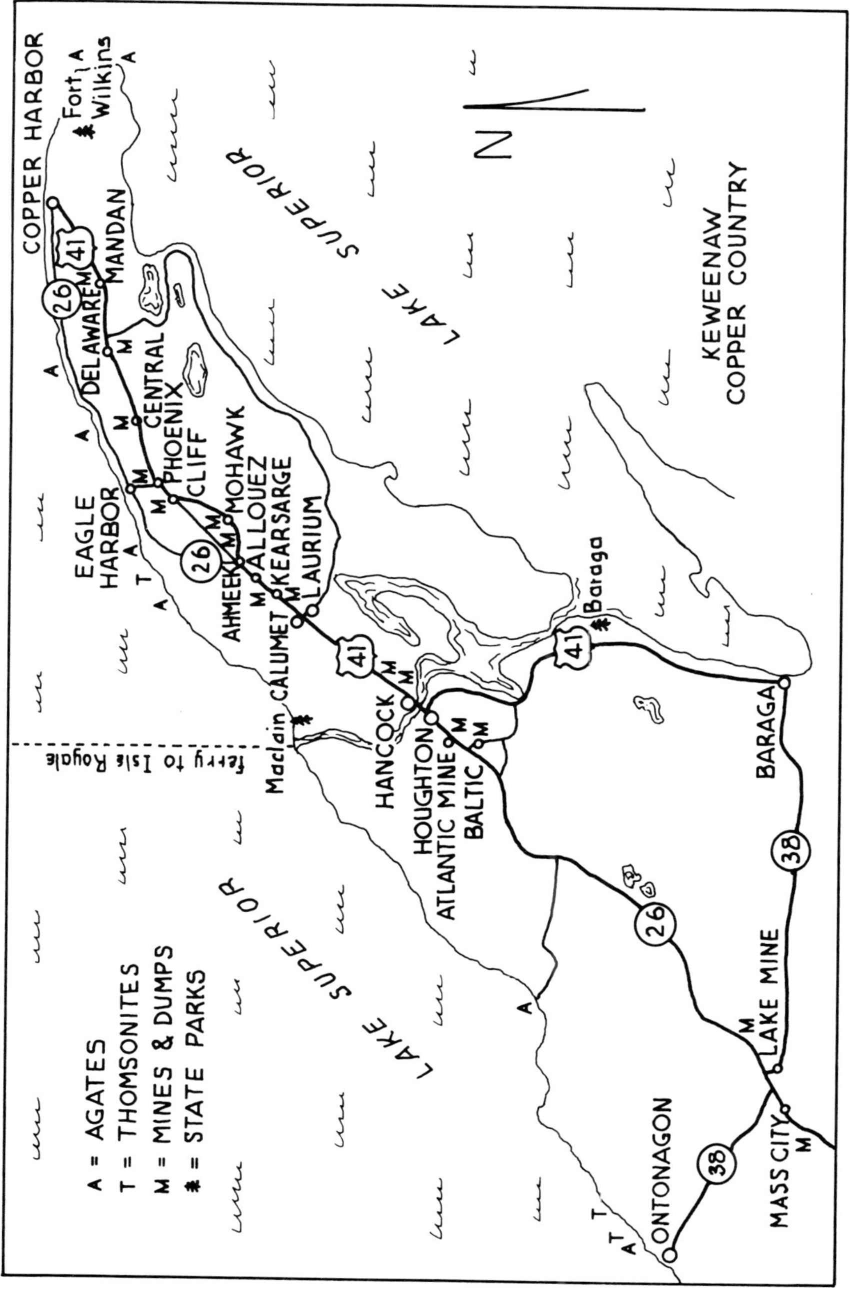

dumps of the historic region in this rock collector's haven. Over 5 million tons of copper were produced in the mines of the Keweenaw Peninsula from 1945 to the time the mines of the Calumet and Hecla closed in 1969. Some of the mines produced mostly native coppers. Many of the old dumps carry rich ores, fine specimens and unusual cutting materials, overlooked in the heyday of the "copper rush". However, old dumps are overgrown and sometimes difficult to find.

The Upper Peninsula copper rush was not only the first rush for the red metal in the United States, but it was the world's largest deposit of native copper, and hundreds of mines were in production, many being worked by European miners who flocked to the new mines.

At present there are only two mines working, both in Ontonagon County: the White Pine and the Caledonia. The White Pine, a leading producer, crushes all ore underground, so there are no waste piles. There are no tours at this mine and collectors should not go there.

The Caledonia was reopened on a small scale in 1986 where exploration and specimen mining are in progress. Recent finds include silver, datolite, calcite, and crystallized copper; the esthetic masses of native copper are

Old copper mines near Eagle River, Keweenaw County, Michigan

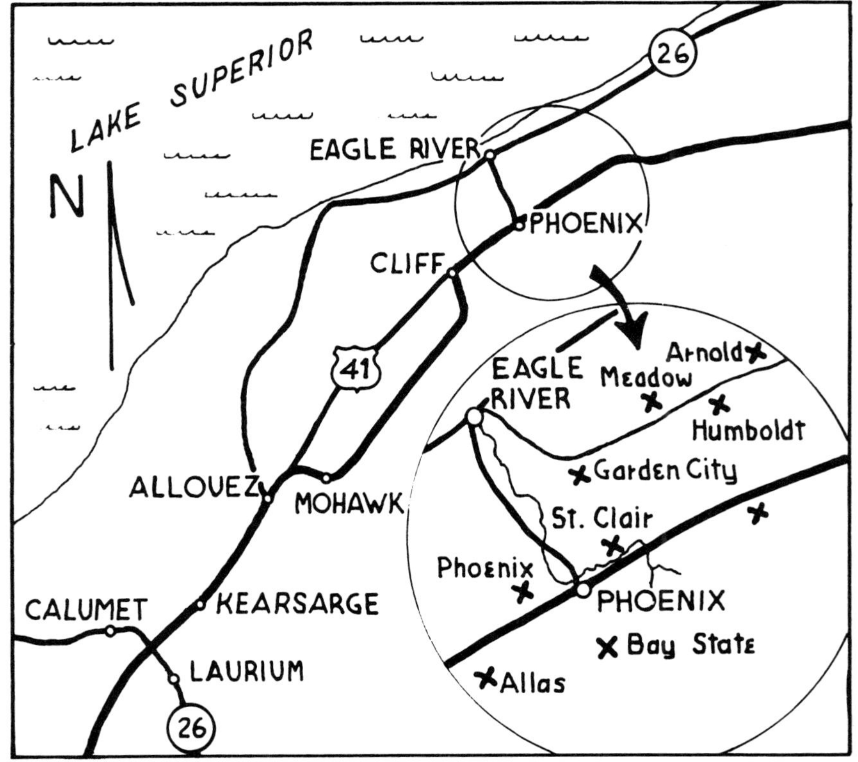

cleaned and sold as decorator specimens. This mine allows collecting trips for organized groups. For details contact Richard Whiteman or Red Metal Mineral Company, Hancock, Michigan.

Over 100 different minerals are known to occur in the waste dumps of old copper mines. Although some are rare, 20 are considered easy to find. Some which the mineral collectors look for are algodonite, ankerite, calcite chlorastrolite, chrysocolla, datolite, epidote, feldspar, malachite, copper, prehnite, quartz, silver, tenorite, thomsonite and such cutting materials as mohawkite, patricianite, copper-bearing epidote, and copper-conglomerate.

Once active mines dot the entire countryside north of Hancock and Houghton in Keweenaw County, with old and dim trails crisscrossing the region. Other dumps are in Houghton and Ontonagon Counties. Bob Williams, a member of the Kalamazoo Club, who spends 6 months or more of each year in the copper peninsula tells about several of the mines and their products.

The Copper Falls Mine is on a county road which turns right from U.S. 41 to Eagle River. From a dirt road going uphill, the first left leads to the overburden pile. Copper, analcite, natrolite, datolite and calcite are among the minerals here.

The Central Mine is next to U.S. 41. The county hauls fill from here, and fine specimens have been uncovered at those times, including copper crystals, prehnite, chlorastrolite, quartz, and datolite.

An excellent mine was the Phoenix, and local contractors sometimes haul rock from this mine dump. The collectable materials from the Phoenix are copper, prehnite, chlorastrolite, calcite and zeolites. The Phoenix Mine is south of Eagle River and just north of U.S. 41.

A storied mine is the Cliff which is also south of Eagle River. The Cliff Mine is about a mile southwest of the Phoenix and just north of U.S. 41. Michigan's State Gem, chlorastrolite can be found here as well as datolite and prehnite. Williams warns the road up the cliff is steep, but the view is beautiful.

The Gratiot Mine is on a county road west of Mohawk. Cuttable apple-green prehnite is found here, as well as some of the unique copper-silver specimens called "half breeds".

The Ojibway Mine has copper, quartz crystals, microcline, calcite and datolite.

Mohawkite is a mineral from the Mohawk Mine. The digging here is hard work, as it is in many of the dumps, with the best rock pile being in back of the White Swan Motel at the north edge of Mohawk on U.S. 41. Bob Williams suggests the use of a metal detector in areas such as this.

The Allouez Mine is north of Calumet on U.S. 41. Turning west at the Amoco Station, you will find the rock piles on the right of the trail up the hill. Chrysocolla and conglomerate occur here.

The Osceola Mine is at Osceola. Copper-silver specimens, calcite, prehnite, and attractive red microcline are found here, and much of the material is of lapidary quality. The copper wire specimens are interesting display minerals.

The Wolverine Mine of Kearsarge has epidote and agate.

Datolite nodules were abundant in the Old Quincy Mine, and were also

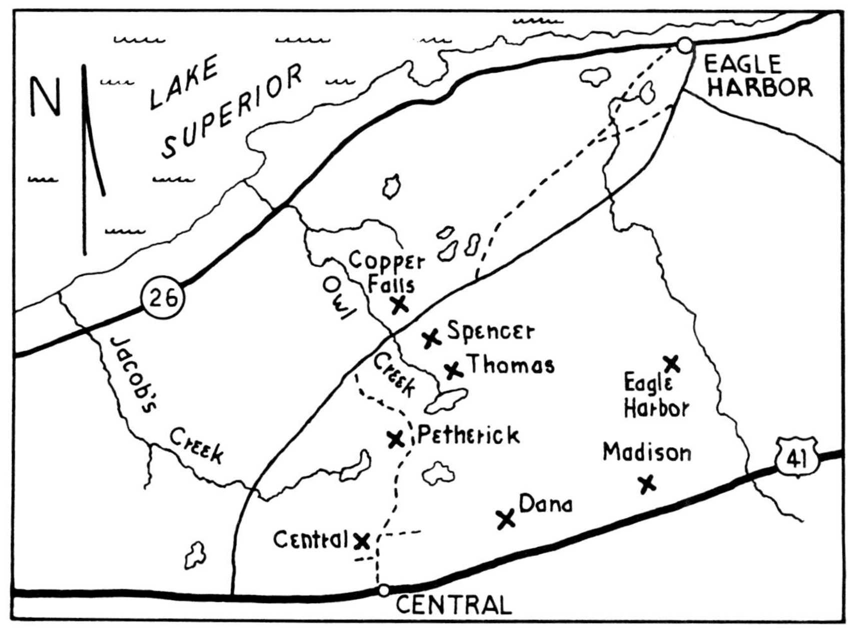

Old copper mines southwest of Eagle Harbor

among the prizes from the Clark, Iroquois Star, Delaware, Copper Falls, Central, Centennial, Lake, and Caledonia Mines. Datolite has also been found in a gravel pit near Mandan, along the shore of Lake Superior at Highrock Bay and off the north shore of Isle Royale, where it has been collected by scuba divers.

Datolite is a gorgeous mineral which occurs in the copper country in irregular nodules up to 6 inches in diameter. The nodules contain finely disseminated native copper, and the colors are wonderful tints of peach, yellow, orange, pink, rose, salmon, old gold, and sometimes green or violet. The material is 5 1/2 in hardness, compact and takes a beautiful porcelain-like polish.

Look for datolite at the Old Quincy at the narrow arm of Portage Lake in Houghton County and the Iroquois Mine north of Houghton. The Clark Mine dumps are 2 miles east of Copper Harbor near the tip of Keweenaw County. Look also in the Delaware Mine near the community of Delaware on Highway 41.

In Ontonagon County the Mass Mine dumps are on Route 26 near the community of Mass.

Cutting quality epidote is quite common on some of the dumps. It occurs in various shades and tints of green and often has inclusions of native copper. Some of the best places to look for epidote are the Osceola Mine, Caledonia, Champion, and Adventure Mines in Ontonagon County and also in the Calumet, Baltic, and Painesville dumps.

Cutting quality prehnite, in lovely jade-like tones, is an occurrence of the Central, Cliff, and Phoenix Mines of Keweenaw County, and the Herwood, Minnesota and Toltec Mines of Ontonagon County.

Nodules of prehnite and thomsonite are found along the shore at the Calumet Waterworks Beach of Houghton County.

There are many other mine dumps throughout the area and many other minerals to look for. Micromounters have a field day here. For larger specimens look for some of the dumps which have been disturbed for road material or for landfill. In such dumps, long buried material is exposed.

Some of the other dumps are Flintsteel, Isle Royale, Michigan, Humboldt, Meadow, Resolute, Kingston, Ahmeek, Stotenburgh, Kelly, Montreal, Copper Harbor, Amygdaloid, and Manganese. Some of the other minerals are melaconite, apophyllite, chalcopyrite, covellite, pyrite, sphalerite, stilbite, azurite, dioptase, hematite heulandite, mesolite, powellite, chlorite, natrolite, magnetite, phillipsite, leonhardite, and iddingsite.

An interesting and productive location is called Thomsonite Hill which is just off a dirt road between the Delaware and Eagle Harbor Mines in Keweenaw County. It overlooks Lake Superior and Eagle Harbor. Under a foot or so of overburden, gem "thomsonites" are found in the decaying basalt, although the small pink nodules have been found to be prehnite with copper inclusions rather than thomsonite. There is a great resemblance in the structure of the prehnite and thomsonite nodules, but prehnite is both harder and heavier than true thomsonite. Thomsonite nodules are also found along Lake Superior.

Quartz is found in many variations on the Keweenaw. Along with the highly prized Lake Superior agate are colorful patterned jaspers, angular breccias, translucent carnelian, sards, plasmas, chalcedonies, and crystalline quartzes in a rainbow of colors.

Look on the beaches near Highway M26 between Eagle River and Eagle Harbor and in the weathered basalt near Copper Harbor. Five Mile Point and Seven Mile Point are good areas. The access to Seven Mile Point is a county

Copper mines east of Eagle Harbor, Keweenaw County

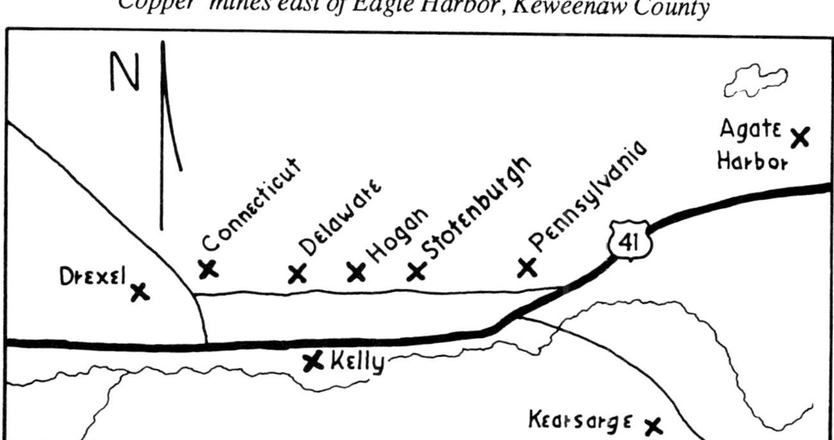

road with a sign reading "Sunset Bay-Calvins". There is a fee here of $1.00 per car. Agates and quartz gems are found for several miles along the beach.

Other locations are Agate Beach, High Rock Bay, Keystone Bay, Fort Wilkins Beach, Horseshoe Harbor, Eagle River, Silver Creek, Black Creek and Gratiot River. Agate is found in place on the north shore of Manganese Lake, a small lake west of the Clark Mine. Blue-green chalcedony called chrysocolla in the gem world has been found in the Allouez and Ahmeek Mines.

The calcites of the copper mines are exceptionally beautiful. Some of the most elegant and showy crystals are pink or red from inclusions of cuprite or copper. Well-formed vivid red crystals have come from Allouez, Copper Falls, Quincy and Centennial Mines. Large lavender calcite crystals are a rare occurrence from the Franklin Mine. Lustrous white and colorless crystals came from the Pewabic Mine. From the Ahmeek Mine, came calcite crystals with copper phantoms. Jet black calcite crystals are a recent find in the Caledonia Mine.

Chlorastrolite is one of the most desired materials of the Lake Superior shores of Michigan. The state gem is a variety of pumpellyite. The literal meaning is "green star". The small gems occur as fillings in basalt and sometimes as beach pebbles. The polygon designs are radial in structure and are encased in green chlorite. When polished, they have a chatoyant luster and a rich deep blue-green color. The best location is Isle Royale which is a National Park, where no collecting is allowed. The gem is also found on the

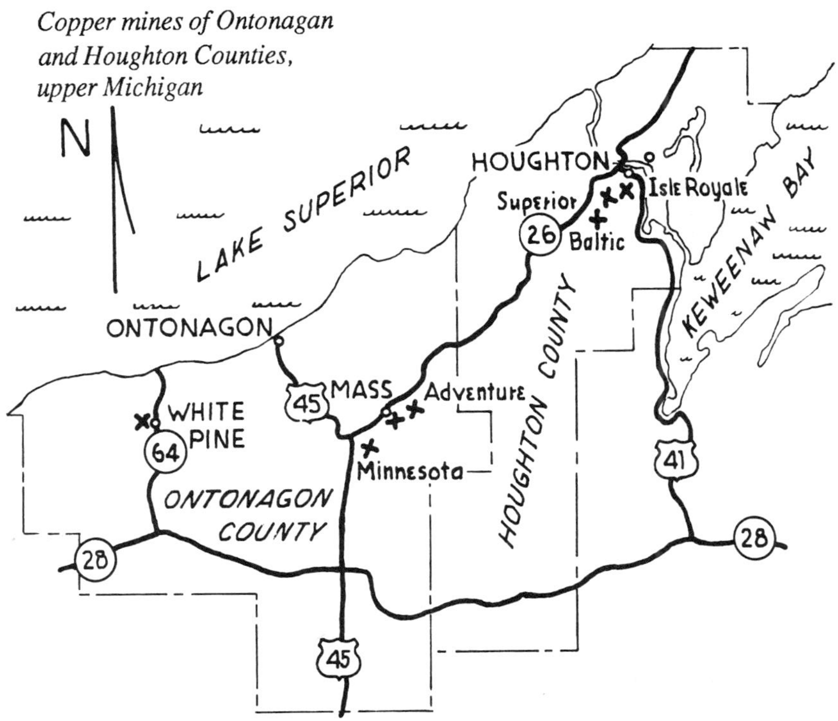

Copper mines of Ontonagan and Houghton Counties, upper Michigan

beaches of Smithwick and Mott Islands. Several mines in the Keweenaw have also yielded specimens.

Another popular cutting material is copper in basalt. The altered red-brown basalt has stringers of bright native copper. Domeykite, a copper arsenide associated with mohawkite and algodonite, is a metallic gem material with white quartz veining. It takes a brilliant metallic polish with iridescent colors. The Mohawk, Ahmeek, Hancock, and Sheldon mines have produced this material.

Copper-nickel arsenides of cutting quality are abundant at the Ahmeek 3 and 4 Mines, south of Mohawk, and at the Mohawk #2 at Mohawk. Some of the other unusual minerals in these mines are rammelsbergite, niccolite and arsenical copper.

Of course native copper has always been the primary attraction of this 200 mile long area. The copper occurs in many esthetic forms. Native copper is red, ductile, malleable, 2.5 in hardness and 8.8 in specific gravity. The luster is metallic and the crystal system is isometric. In Michigan there are lacy arborescent specimens, twister wire copper, distorted crystals of sculptured shapes, and sometimes copper pseudomorphs. There are copper "skulls", copper nuggets, copper veins, dendritic copper, copper shells, copper spikes, unique copper-silver "half breeds", and copper boulders.

Indian hammerstones have been found near many of the mines, proving that the Indians worked this area for copper for spears, arrowheads, tools and

Prize-winning specimens of datolite show black and copper veining against a soft, glowing pink. From the Harry Sprague collection. Photo – Dr. Oliver Lohr

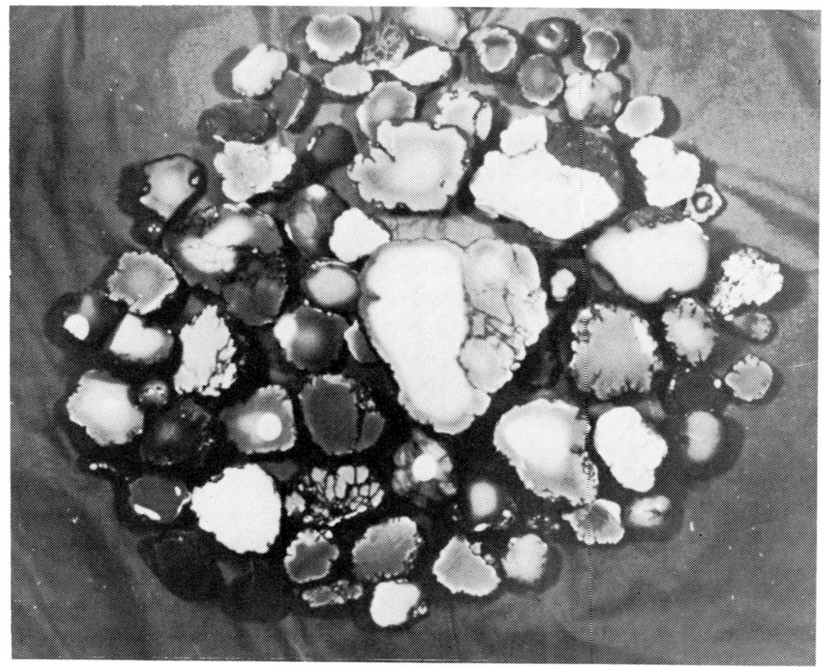

ornaments. Native copper projectile points have been found great distances from the copper country.

The largest mass of pure copper was over 500 tons, found in Ontonagon County in the Minnesota Mine. The Indians worshipped a 3,000 pound copper mass found on the Ontonagon River. It was transported by glacier from its original location. The first white men saw this gigantic boulder in 1765, although by then some had already been carried away. Early copper hunters tried to fracture the mass by fire. Eventually Julius Eldred of Detroit was able to purchase rights to the Ontonagon Boulder after a series of frustrating delays. He expected to set it up in Detroit as a commercial attraction and had already started to move it on its long journey, when it was seized by the U.S. War Department. It finally got to Detroit and was shown there for less than a month, when the U.S. District Attorney ordered it to be shipped to Washington D.C. by boat. It is now in the Smithsonian in the U.S. Museum of Natural Science.

It is best to consult with Bob Williams of the Copper Country Mineral Club, Arnold Mulzer of the Ishpeming Club or other hobbyists before collecting in upper Michigan.

Upper Michigan has three iron ranges, the Gogebic, mostly in Gogebic County, the Marquette of Marquette County and the Menominee of Dickinson and Iron Counties. Best known to collectors is the area around Marquette and Ishpeming. The Chambers of Commerce in both cities have current information for collectors, and in both places, there are fine collections of local materials on display,

Mineral locations in Baraga and Marquette Counties, iron mines in Iron County and the Kona Hills dolomite location

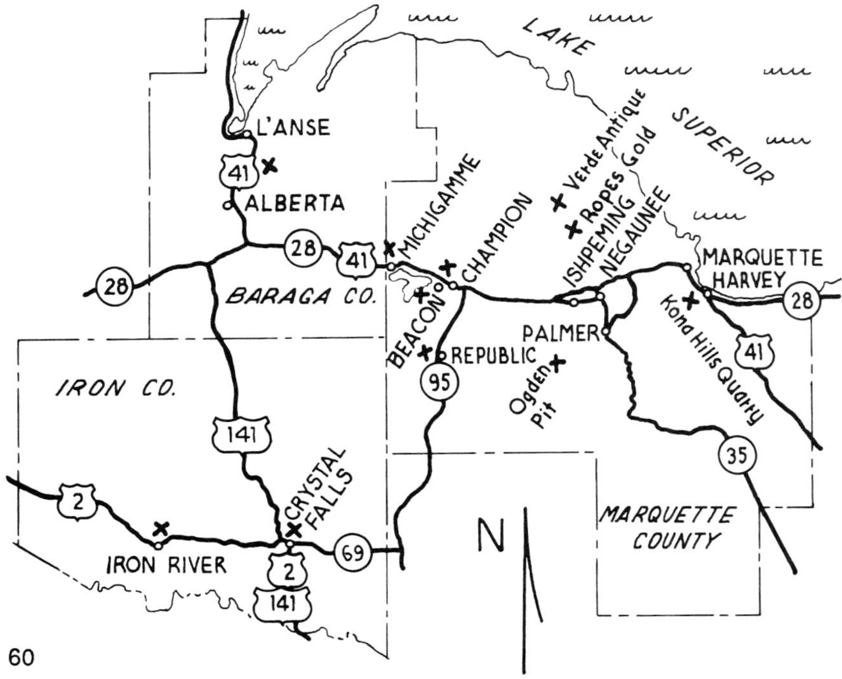

Mine dumps near Marquette, Ishpeming, Michigamee, Republic, Champion, Deer River, Harvey and Presque Isle have produced an amazing variety of cutting material and mineral specimens from mines which yielded many tons of iron ore. Some of the attractive minerals of the Marquette Range are goethite, hematite, chalcopyrite, pyrite, quartz, calcite, dolomite, gypsum, barite, garnet, rhodonite, psilomelane, siderite, talc, staurolite, tourmaline, serpentine, verde antique and gold.

The Lindberg quarry near Marquette has been a bountiful area for exotic Kona dolomite, a striking cutting material of subtle colors and graceful patterns, named for the Kona Hills. There are exposures of this cherty dolomitic rock in cuts, quarries, and excavations from east of Goose Lake, through the Ragged Hills, and north to Tigo Lake, and east to the Lake Superior shore. Another deposit is located from Mount Chocolay to Mount Mesnard, Morgan Furnace and Teal Lake. However most of the lapidary material has been obtained from the Lindberg quarry and others. The hardest and most colorful material is difficult to find, since the productive quarry is an old one which has been extensively hunted.

The colors of the dolomite are off-white, ivory, buff, mauve, pink, brown, and light green. The patterns are in geometric veins or brecciated. Some pieces are reminiscent of Oriental art.

A vivid red jasper banded with glistening metallic specular hematite is a distinctive gemstone from this part of Michigan. Called jaspilite, it is found near Michigamee, Negaunee, the Porcupine Mountains, and several other places in the iron range. The classic outcrop is Jasper Hill at Ishpeming where the

The gold area of northern Michigan

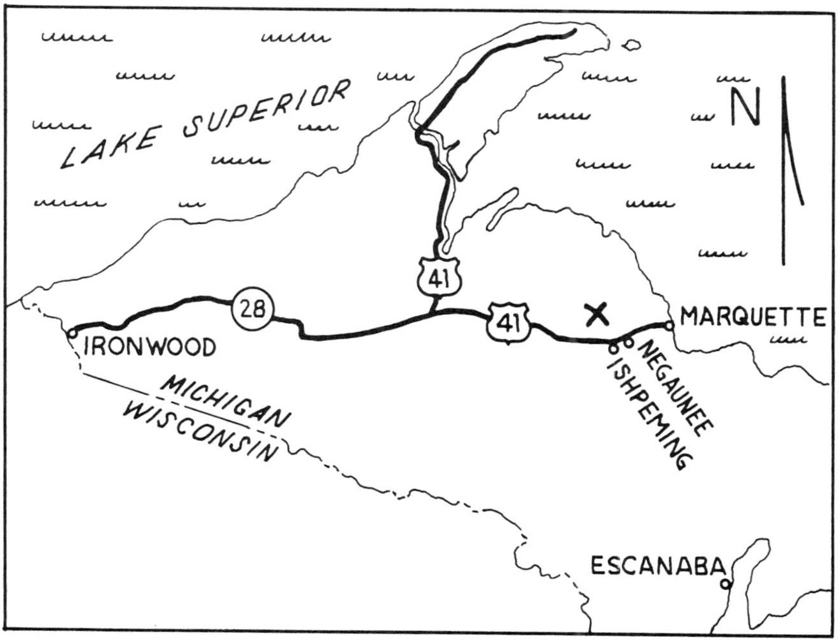

Ishpeming Club has made plans to preserve the bright beautiful rock hill. The same material can be obtained in places which are not landmarks, such as the Republic Mine and Palmer. Bob Markert of Ishpeming has made many impressive items from Kona dolomite, jaspilite, and other northern Michigan lapidary materials.

Attractive garnet-chloride pseudomorphs are found in several places. The Mt. Shasta location is considered dangerous and is closed, however you may look for the "pseudos" at the Champion and Old Spur Mines.

The Ogden Pit on Cliff's Drive south of Ishpeming has fine quality banded hematite and is also considered a productive spot for micromounters who may also find their tiny treasures in the Jackson and Ohio Mines. The Lucy Mine had some of the finest barite crystals ever found in the state.

Polishable green serpentine called verde antique is found at the mine of the same name. It is mottled and streaked with calcite and dolomite. The reactivation of the nearby Ropes Gold Mine may cut off access to the serpentine mine.

Other minerals found in the iron ranges are pyrolusite, rutile, grunerite, marcasite, manganite, rhodochrosite, talc and tourmaline.

An unusual occurrence of selenite was discovered in Iron County where a flooded mine was dewatered, and the saturated workings, walls, and floors were found to be covered with long and exquisite selenite crystals.

Quartz crystals, crimson in color because of iron inclusions, have been spectacular Iron County finds. Staurolite has been found at the Peavy Dam on the Michigamee River, and agates are found in glacial gravels.

Upper Michigan is a fantastic area for collectors, but the best spots are becoming inaccessible. The area must be treated with respect by all field collectors who must cooperate with the hospitable club members of the area in keeping these areas open for generations to enjoy.

Lower Michigan

The star of lower Michigan is undoubtedly the Petoskey stone, the treasured State Stone of Michigan, found over an extensive part of the upper segment of lower Michigan from Traverse Bay to Alpena. Although a popular cutting material, Petoskey stone is calcite, not quartz. An intricately patterned fossil coral of the Devonian Period, it is distinguished by its honeycomb-like structure and contrasting radial markings. Specimens range in size from pebbles to large masses, but the most cuttable are those from about 2 inches to 5 inches in diameter. The colors range from light beige, ecru, tan, gray, and buff to deep brown and charcoal shades. The real Petoskey stone is Hexagonaria, but similarly preserved fossil corals of other species, such as favosites, are also widespread and equally polishable.

Typical Petoskey stones are found as water-worn rounded specimens on the beaches along the south shore of Little Traverse Bay from the city of Petoskey to Charlevoix, in road cuts, quarries, gravel piles, and excavations. They are also found along Torch Lake, Burt Lake and others. Unweathered

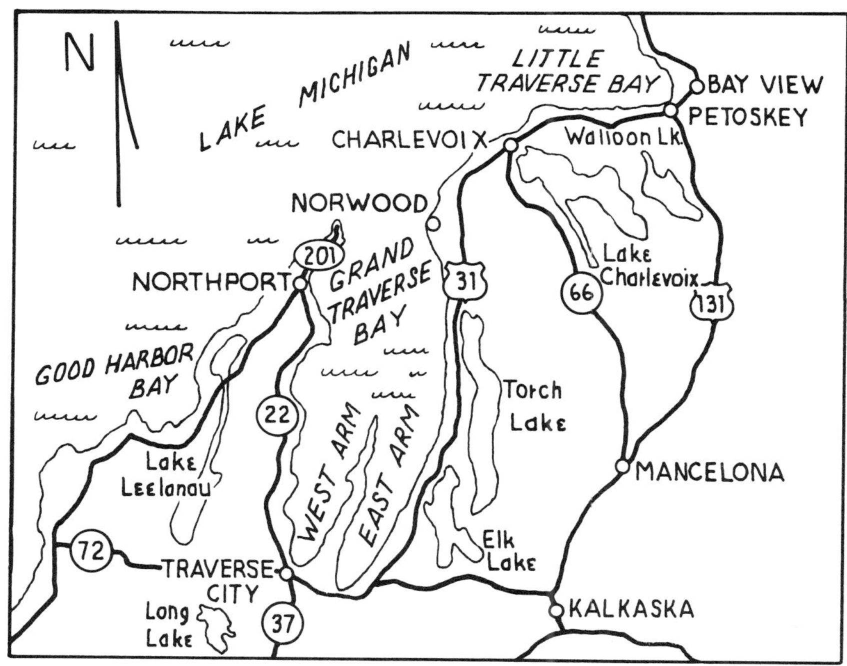

Petoskey stones and other fossils are found on these lake shores and in quarries in this area

specimens in quarries are easier to recognize in the rough than water-worn ones, because the worn beach stones blend in with all of the other beach materials. On the beaches it is easier to find good specimens when it is raining.

The corals of the lower peninsula are two general types, solitary corals and colony corals. The fossil corals of Michigan all belong to extinct species.

Solitary corals belong to the tetracorals, a typical example being the large rugose coral Siphonophrentis. Cystiphillum and Ptychophyllum are other Devonian rugose corals. Horn corals or cup corals are Heterophrentis or Zaphrentis.

A branching type of colony coral is Coenites. It is Devonian, while the chain coral Halysites is Silurian. The Silurian favosites called the honeycomb coral is composed of small geometric corallites.

Another tabulate coral in this group is Syringopora, which has been given the common name organ pipe coral because of its symmetrical parallel pipes.

Lithostrotionella is found in quarries and is sometimes confused with Hexagonaria, which is the true "Petoskey stone".

Another Michigan coral is Aulopora michiganesnsis, obviously named for the state where it was discovered. It is a Devonian coral found in the Traverse Bay area. Aulopora consists of small tubes branching in divergent directions in thick wrinkled walls.

Aranchnophyllum is a tetracoral with geometric patterns which at first glance resemble lithostrotionella. Found in these same locations are

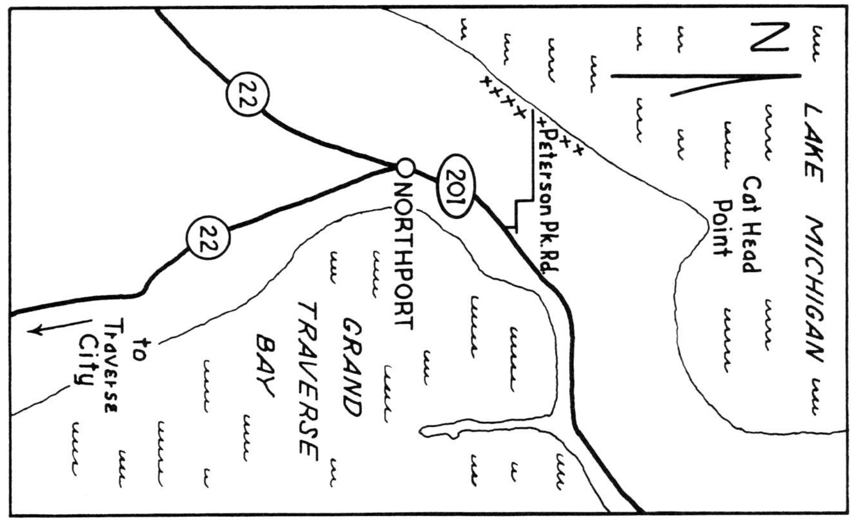

Petoskey stones and fossils southwest of Cat Head Point near Peterson Park

Stromatoporoids which are extinct coral-like marine organisms which built up irregular limy masses in the coral reefs.

Petoskey stones have been found in Emmet, Charlevoix, Antrim, Cheboygan, Presque Isle, Alpena, Grand Traverse and Leelanau Counties. A good location is provided by William Clark of the Grand Travers area rock club, This is the Peterson Park Christmas Cove area west of Northport, Leelanau County. Take Route M201 north of Northport 1 1/4 miles and turn left on the Peterson Park Road. The park is 2 1/2 miles farther west. Besides the fossil corals beach combing on the public beach may reveal epidote, unakite and conglomerate. There are Devonian pelecypods on the northeast shore of North Fox Island, Leelanau County.

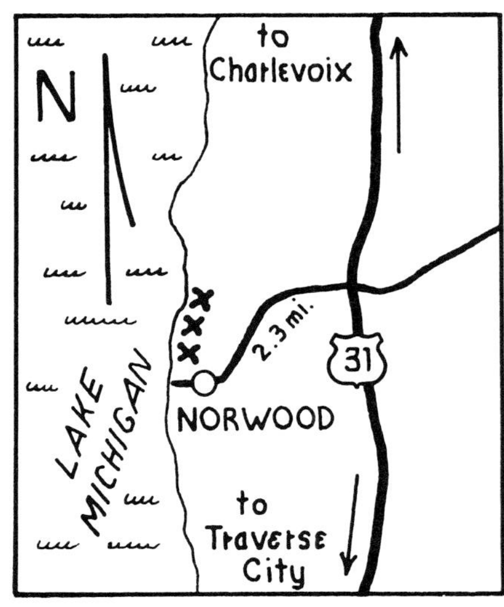

Location for banded chert in Charlevoix County

Another good location for Petoskey stones and similar fossils, is south of Ironton on the east side of Highway 66. This is an abandoned gravel pit. Also in Charlevoix County is another old gravel pit on the north side of the road from East Jordan to Ellsworth, which has furnished collectors with many species.

The Medusa Quarry near Traverse City allows clubs to collect the rich-looking brown Petoskey stones there.

In Charlevoix County, Devonian pelecypods and corals are found 3/4 mile northeast of the Beaver Island Coast Guard Station on northeast Beaver Island. They are also found in ledges and bluffs at Pine River Point on Lake Michigan. Other fossil locations are 1 1/2 miles north of Norwood and the southeast point of Trout Island. The beach area north of Norwood also has a colorful banded chert which is cuttable, as well as Petoskey stones.

Kitty Starbuck, editor of the Kalamazoo Geological Society's bulletin "Gems" advises collectors that the best material may be hidden among the rocks at the water's edge. She also mentions the Lake Michigan beach just west of Torch Lake in Antrim County. Kitty is active in the excellent shows of the Kalamazoo club and the Midwest Federation, as well as their field trips and educational activities.

Fossils are abundant at Rogers City, Presque Isle County, in the large limestone quarry there. Gastropods locally called "petrified snails" are among the fossils. Calcite crystals are also found here. In this same county fossil corals occur 4 miles east of Liske and 1 mile east of Trout Creek in road cuts on U.S. 23. Other corals are located 9 miles east of Rogers City east of Swan Creek in a road cut on New Shore Road.

Amateurs have found several new species and even new genera of fossils in the quarries of Michigan's lower peninsula. A good example of a new genus of sponge of the Devonian Period was found by Pat Rutkowski in the famous quarry at Alpena, Alpena County. This immense and important quarry, 3 miles by 2 miles, still allows visitors, and sharp-eyed and knowledgeable collectors are still contributing to science by their finds here. Alpena Petoskey stone is black. Crystals of calcite, dolomite, and ankerite occur in the quarry vugs. South of Alpena at Squaw Bay, there are concretions with pyrite and marcasite. The Alpena coastline is on Lake Huron. Old quarries are at Rockport and Devils Lake. Other Alpena County locations are Four Mile Dam, Ferron Point, and Thunder Bay.

There is good collecting for fossil plants in the following Michigan Counties: Monroe, Alpena, Presque Isle, and Delta. Look on shoreline exposures, road cuts, railroad cuts, old abandoned quarries, and new construction excavations, the best places to look being where the Paleozoic bedrock is on the surface, or near it, and where there has been considerable weathering.

The fossil plants are mostly from the Pennsylvanian Period, although some may be from the Devonian.

Lepidodendron, an extinct club moss tree, is sometimes found in broken pieces of trunk casts in sandstone, showing the distinctive leaf scars. Stigmaria, thought to be the root section of Lepidodendron, and Sigillaria another of the club moss trees are also present in these areas.

Delicate carbonized fern leaves occur on Pennsylvanian shale, which may be Neuropteris, a seed fern. Imprints of fern fronds such as Pectopteris are found in some exposures.

A close relative of the modern horsetail, the fragile-appearing Asterophyllites prints, occur in Pennsylvanian outcrops.

Sandstone casts of Calamites, also a horsetail type of plant with bamboo-like joints, are other possible finds along with Cordiates, an extinct tree.

It is important to wrap each fossil plant carefully and keep a record of exactly where it was found.

Another county on Lake Huron with numerous collectables is Huron County. Showy calcite crystals with iridescent pyrite have been found at a quarry near Pigeon, and pyrite nodules have been found in black shale. Interesting concentric nodules of chert, siderite and sometimes galena have been found in quarries. The Wallace Stone Quarry off Highway 142 near Bayport yields esthetic crystals, among them calcite, celestite and pyrite. Rare millerite nodules are a special prize here. Cephalopods are found near the lighthouse at Point aux Barques and a Fat Rock Point.

Selenite, alabaster, and gypsum occur in several places in lower Michigan. Some of the rock beds are exposed in Arenac, Iosco and Kent Counties. (A city in Iosco County is even named Alabaster.)

The most famous of the gypsum locations is in Grand Rapids, Kent County, where the mines have produced pink, white, and red alabaster and huge clear selenite crystals, and veins of chatoyant "satin spar". The old Grand Rapids Gypsum Mine is now operated by the Michigan Natural Storage Company, and collecting is allowed on a fee basis. Some of the tunnels, 85 feet below the surface, are used as cold rooms for bulk storage. In the

Alabaster fee area at Grand Rapids, Michigan

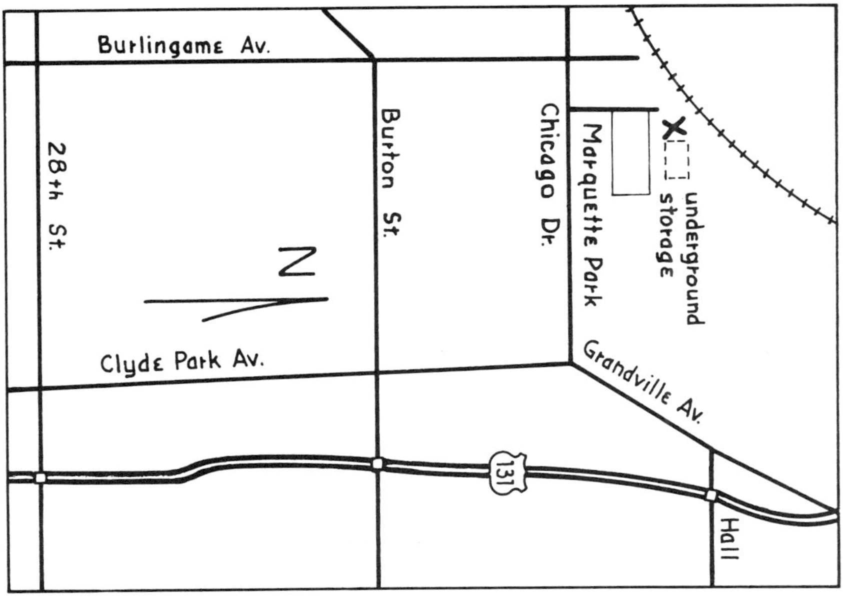

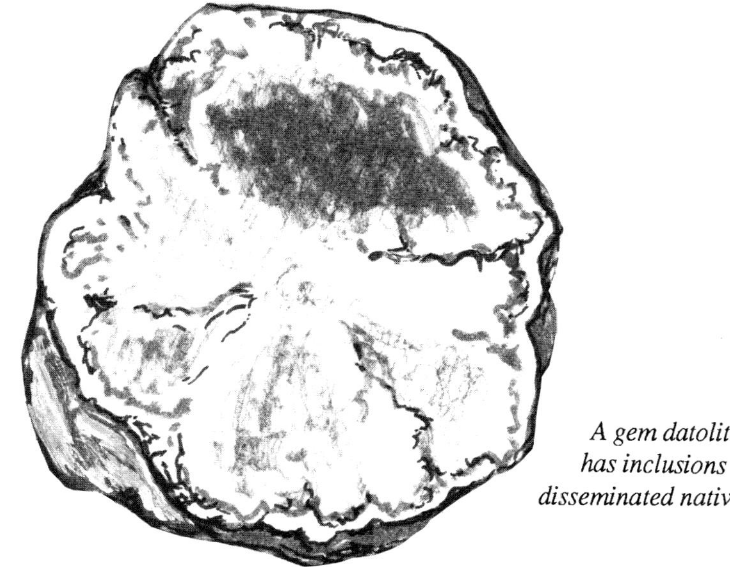

A gem datolite nodule has inclusions of finely disseminated native copper

collecting area, the alabaster layer is from 7 to 10 feet thick, with other areas of massive clear, colorless selenite. There are crystals on the ceiling and in cavities. Robert Beauvais, Assistant State Director of the Midwest Federation, writes that visitors to the mine should wear warm clothing, as the mine is a constant 55 degrees. Take a good portable light source, heavy hammers, sledges, chisels, and wrapping materials. Michigan field trippers add hot coffee and lunch to their supplies and make a day of it.

The address of the Storage Company-mine is 1200 Judd Southwest. From Highway U.S. 131 turn west at 28th Street to Burlingame. Turn north here to Chicago Street, then three blocks to Judd. The office is south of the railroad track.

North of Imlay City in Lapeer County puddingstone conglomerate and fossils are found. Conglomerate is found in many of the quarries and gravel pits near Lake Huron in the region known as "Michigan's thumb".

The Cheney Quarry in Bellevue, Eaton County, has attracted field enthusiasts who are interested in showy mineral specimens. The marcasite is iridescent, the calcite is snowy white, and the pyrite is bright. There are also sphalerites, celestites and fluorites. The quarry is open to collecting on weekends. Bellevue is north of Battle Creek on a state route west of Interstate 69.

Ironstone concretions containing siderite, galena, marcasite, pyrite, and sphalerite occur at the Eaton Quarry north of Lansing and Grand Ledge.

Wayne County is densely populated. Detroit, the great automobile city, also produces the salt which rusts out their product. The International Salt Company started mining in 1910. The salt is interbedded with anhydrite in a layer 450 feet thick. (This is not a collecting area). Some of the minerals found in Wayne County excavations are quartz, pyrite, celestite, dolomite and hematite. Fossils are also found.

Monroe County has several excellent quarries which are closed to collectors at present. Geodes, beautiful crystals, and excellent fossils have been taken from these quarries. The quarries known to be closed are at Monroe, Scofield, and Rockwood. Collecting continues at Milan in a quarry 1/4 mile off the county road. The quarry is flooded, but behind it there are extensive dumps where there are excellent trilobites, brachiopods, bryzoans, corals, gastropods, crinoids, pelecypods and other fossils. There are also quarries at Ottawa Lake, Petersburg, Dundee and Plum Creek. Inquire locally about access to Monroe County quarries.

A single diamond has been recorded for Michigan. It is the Dowagiac diamond found in Cass County north of the city of Dowagiac. It weighed 10.875 carats. Freshwater pearls have been taken from mollusks in the Detroit, Cass and Rouge Rivers and others, and from rivers in the Keweenaw Peninsula.

Michigan has more clubs than any other state except California. The enthusiastic clubs have many educational activities and produce top-rated shows, the Detroit show being recognized as one of the best three in the nation. The Michigan Mineralogical Society is over 50 years old and is actively involved with the superb Cranbrook Museum. Many hobby leaders come from Michigan clubs. Some of the shows to see are Kalamazoo, Flint, Dearborn, Lansing, Jackson, Grand Rapids, Holland, Plymouth and Benton Harbor. The Harbor. The Michigan Geology and Gemcraft Society produces a unique earth science and lapidary educational seminar each spring.

Excellent mineral and fossil exhibits may be seen at Cranbrook, the University of Michigan, Michigan State, and at educational institutions in Adrian, Alma, Battle Creek, Hillsdale, and Grand Rapids. There are also museums at Three Oaks and Kalamazoo. The Seaman Museum at Michigan Tech in Houghton is a noted mineral museum, with accents on the magnificent copper country specimens.

There are many important mineral, gem, and fossil dealers, lapidary suppliers, and manufacturers in Michigan. Some of these are located in Ann Arbor, Bay City, Belleville, Beulah, Birmingham, Brooklyn, Charlotte, Copper Harbor, Grand Blanc, Harbor Springs, Ironwood, Jackson, Kalamazoo, Kewadin, Lapeer, Norway, Roseville, Royal Oak, Sanford, Southgate, Sterling Heights, Warren, and Wixom.

It is important to contact members of the Michigan Clubs before making a long trip there to do everything possible to plan such a trip well. Determine the status of the areas you wish to visit, and when you get there, do everything possible to keep all productive localities open for the future.

Beach stones from upper Michigan include jaspers, agates and other quartzes

Michigan's gem, chlorastrolite, is found in basalt matrix

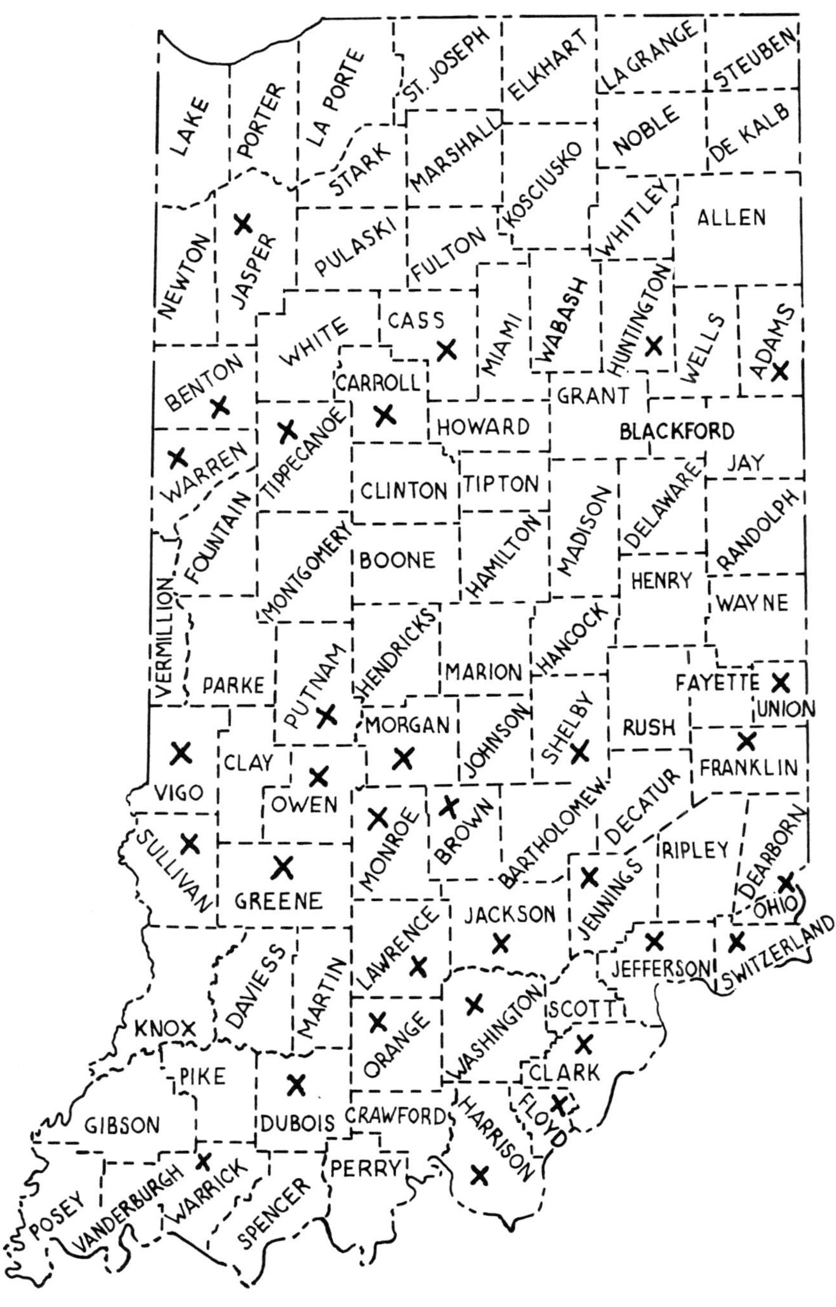

Major Indiana mineral and fossil counties

INDIANA

Indiana is a highly industrialized state, but it is an agricultural state as well. There are scores of quarries in this state where limestone is important enough to be the State Rock. About two-thirds glaciated, Indiana drift has yielded such surprises as over 30 diamonds. There are many coal mines in western Indiana and oil fields in several parts of the state. The state also produces clay and gypsum. The southern part of Indiana, rich in scenery and history, is the most interesting to mineral collectors. Fossils are abundant in many counties, but there is very little in the way of gem material in the state.

Northern Indiana

Very unusual pyrite is just one of the many happy finds at the Pleasant Ridge Quarry near Rensselaer, Jasper County's prime collecting site. The quarry is 5 miles east of Rensselaer on Indiana Route 114 and immediately west of Pleasant Ridge. Calcite, marcasite, and sphalerite are among the interesting crystals here.

Barite can be found near Remington in Benton County, on outcrops along Carpenter Creek. Barite and aragonite occur near Fowler in cuts along Big Pine Creek.

Cass County has furnished crystal collectors with attractive specimens of apatite, calcite, marcasite and quartz from a quarry 2 1/2 miles east of Logansport. Also found here are glauconite, goethite and fossils. Another quarry 4 1/2 miles east of Logansport on Highway 24 has fossil corals.

On the east edge of Huntington, in Huntington County, crystals of

An Indiana quarry for pyrite and crystals

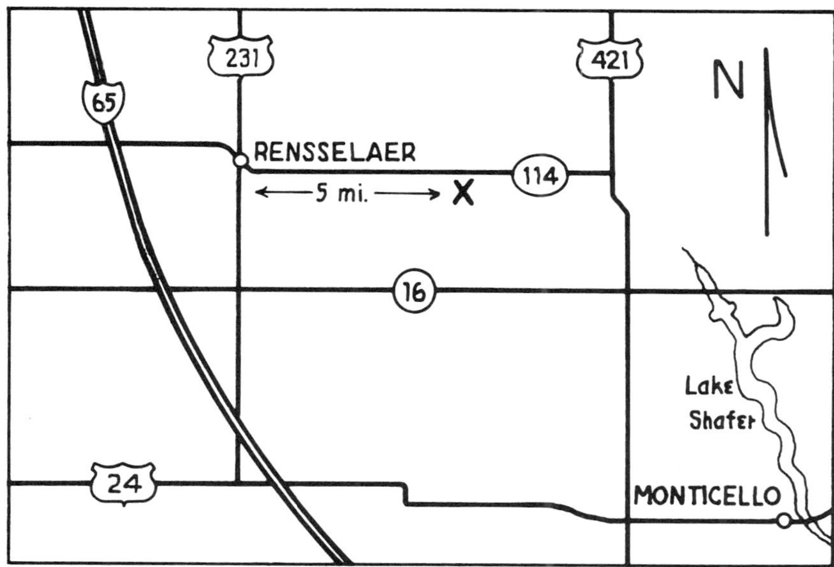

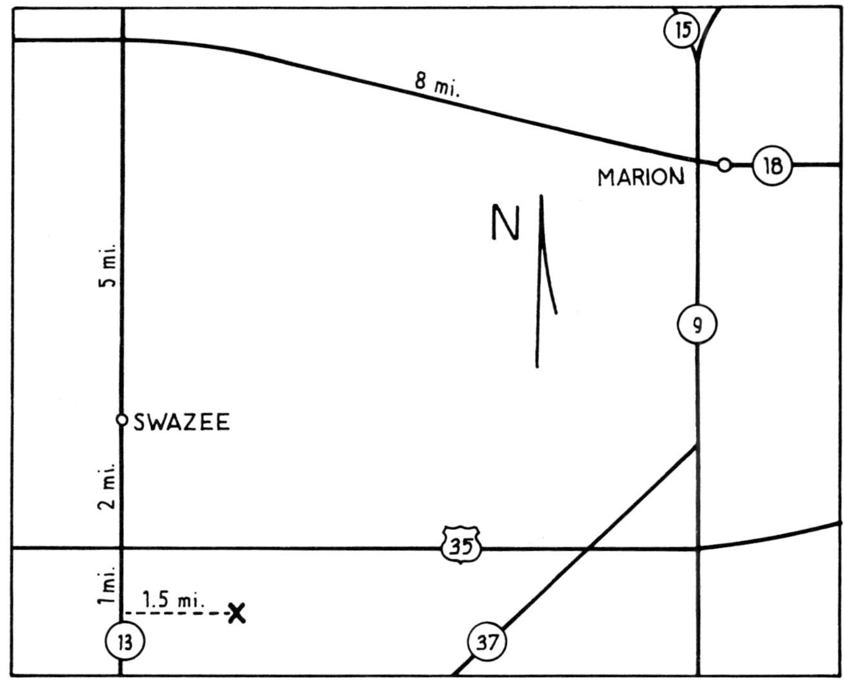

Pipe Creek Quarry fossils and crystals southeast of Swazee, Grant County

calcite, dolomite, marcasite, pyrite, sphalerite and quartz are found in the quarry walls.

Northern Indiana gravels have a variety of materials, although quartz varieties are not common. Gravels are exposed along Wabash in Huntington County and also in Adams County. A gravel pit operator reported that he saves good quartz pebbles, but that he thought this type of material made up only about 1% to 4% of most gravel accumulations. He had white quartz, green quartz, blue quartz, gray quartz, chalcedony, yellow and brown chert, orange quartzite, and a few agates.

Fossils and crystals occur in the Pine Creek Quarry south of Swayzee in Grant County. The access is 1 mile south of U.S. 35 and 1 1/2 miles east of Indiana 13. Get permission.

A fossil coral reef is found in Carroll County near Delphi. The Wabash River between Huntington and Delphi has many natural exposures of Silurian reef fossils. Trilobites and cephalopods are among the fossils to be collected here.

There are several gravel deposits in Tippecanoe and Warren Counties. Sphalerite has been found near Rainsville, and south of West Lebanon.

Indiana collectors enjoy panning for gold in several scenic rivers and tributary streams. Gold has been taken from Sugar Creek west of Crawfordsville in Montgomery County.

Quarries in this county at New Ross, Parkersburg and Waveland have barite, marcasite, melantlerite, quartz and millerite. The shining needle-like crystals of millerite were found matted in hollow crinoid stems.

Near Crawfordsville in this county there is a famous location for Mississippian fossils. Collecting for intricate and esthetic crinoids is possible where streams or excavations have cut through the thick Pleistocene surface deposits. Some of the creeks with Mississippian exposures are Sugar Creek, Indian Creek, South Walnut Fork, and Big Racoon Creek. Museums around the world have crinoid specimens from this county. The land is privately owned and permission must be obtained.

Southern Indiana

The counties below Indianapolis, in southcentral Indiana, are an Eden for collectors. These counties are drained by the White River which joins the Wabash in the southwest corner of the state. Gold and diamonds have been found in these counties, and for those looking for things more easily found, there are geodes by the bushel.

Geode-producing counties of southern Indiana are Monroe, Brown, Lawrence, Jackson, Orange, Washington, Clark, and Floyd. The geodes of Indiana have many shapes and a multitude of inclusions. Easily the most intriguing are the geodes which are shaped exactly like brachiopods, gastropods, pelecypods, crinoids, or other marine fossils. Called "geodized fossils" or "fossilized geodes", these strange objects are buff, white, or off-white, irregular and lumpy on the surface and often much larger than one would expect for the kind of fossil they have replaced. They appear at a glance as if the fossils had been blown up and then frozen. Many of them reveal at once just what marine life started them in this particular direction, but

Locations for gold, geodes, fossils and even diamonds in southcentral Indiana

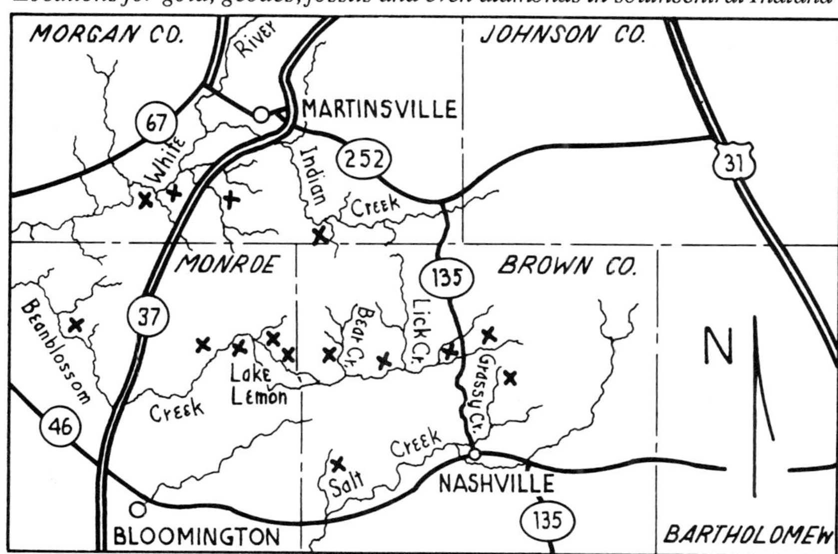

others present puzzles which cannot easily be explained. On the inside, most of the geodes are lined with quartz crystals, resembling those of Iowa, Missouri and Illinois.

Some of the inclusions in the Indiana geodes are calcite, dolomite, chalcedony, barite, marcasite, pyrite, strontianite, galena celestite, selenite, aragonite, fluorite, goethite, limonite and millerite. Colors of inclusions are yellow, orange, brown, blue, gray, black, and pink. Crystals such as galena or pyrite enhance the geodes with their metallic gleam.

Best known of the geode localities of Indiana is Brown County. A popular collecting site for many years has been Bean Blossom Creek north of Nashville, a creek which has also given thrills of discovery to gold panners. More gold and diamonds have been found in Brown County and adjoining Morgan County than in any other location in Indiana.

Geodes are found in road cuts and hillsides near Brown County State Park and around Monroe Lake and Lake Lemon. Lands around the lakes are privately owned. Geodes are also found in portions of the Hoosier National Forest. Some of the lake areas reach into Monroe, Lawrence and Jackson Counties.

Some of the geodes are spherical in shape like the geodes of Iowa, Illinois, and Missouri. Not all of the geodes are hollow and they range in size from 1 inch to 2 feet or more in diameter. They weather out of limestone and dolomite beds and sometimes sandstone or shale. In parts of southern Indiana, geodes are so numerous that they are used for rock gardens, walls, borders, and foundations.

Aragonite, goethite and quartz have been collected from a road cut on

Barite, calcite, dolomite and quartz found in road cuts north and south of Harrodsburg and in a quarry one mile west of Smithville, as well as fossils in a quarry one mile north of Harrodsburg and south of the State Recreation area

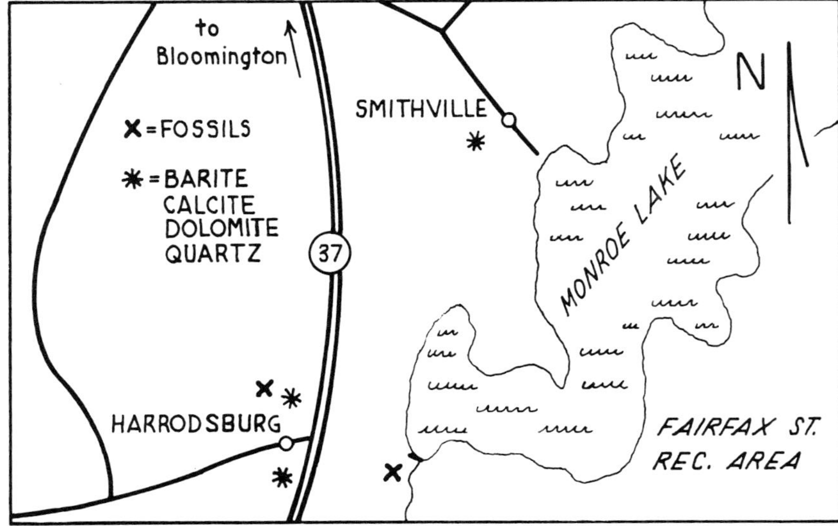

Indiana Highway 46, 2 miles southwest of Nashville, north of the entrance to Brown County State Park.

In Owen County, quartz, siderite and sphalerite are found near Gosport. Try the secondary road 2 miles north of Gosport and the railroad cut southeast of Gosport. An abandoned quarry at the junction of Indiana 46 and the secondary road to Gosport, 4 miles east of Spencer, has specimens of barite, marcasite, pyrite and siderite. Gypsum is found 1 mile southwest of Spencer.

Greene County has a location for gypsum and goethite 1 mile southwest of Switz City. Although there once was a mention of gold in Greene County, the "gold" one is more likely to find here today is "fool's gold" or iron pyrite. The fossils near Jasonville are replaced by pyrite. Fossils include clams, snails, crinoids and other Pennsylvanian sea dwellers. Petrified wood is also found in Greene County.

Barite is found in several places in Lawrence County at locations west of Springville, northwest of Leesville, northeast of Bedford, west of Williams, and west of Georgia. Other minerals found in the limestone of this county are dolomite, strontianite, gypsum, sphalerite calcite, quartz, goethite and millerite. A major industry for Lawrence County and its neighbors is the quarrying of a renowned building stone, the Mississippian "Salem limestone". This hard, gray, beige, tan, and buff dimension stone has been used for many public buildings, educational institutions, memorials and even sculptures. One of the buildings made from this notable deposit is the Empire State Building in New York City. The quarrying operations are centered in Bedford, Oolitic, and Bloomington.

Jackson County has pockets of crystals in the limestone quarries near the town of Medora. Barite, dolomite, marcasite, pyrite, sphalerite, and siderite have been found. Geodes are found in several Jackson County exposures, and old quarries have marine fossils of the Mississippian. One location is 3 miles west of Medora.

Lovely crystals of shining pink dolomite are found in septarian concretions in Jennings County on the northeast edge of North Vernon. Fine crystal specimens of barite, dolomite, calcite, glauconite, pyrite and sphalerite from this area are prizes in many collectors' cabinets. South and west of Vernon, crinoids and other Silurian fossils are found.

Geodes are found in Orange and Washington Counties. They abound in stream banks, excavations, road cuts and quarries in the Salem area of Washington County. Look along the banks of roads and creeks and in quarry walls, both east and west of Salem. Another productive locality is Pekin. Petrified wood has also been found in Washington County exposures, and some of the fine mineral specimens found in this county are fluorite, barite, celestite, gypsum, aragonite and quartz. A barite location is just north of Plattburg with sphalerite being found on the south edge of Harristown. Pyrite occurs in a creek 1 3/4 miles northwest of Salem. Gypsum and sphalerite crystals occur west of Pekin, while other exposures may contain barite and fluorite. Indiana Highways 60 and 135 are access routes to some of these locations.

Abandoned quarries in Washington County are good places to look for mineral specimens. Some are about 1 mile south of Salem and others a mile

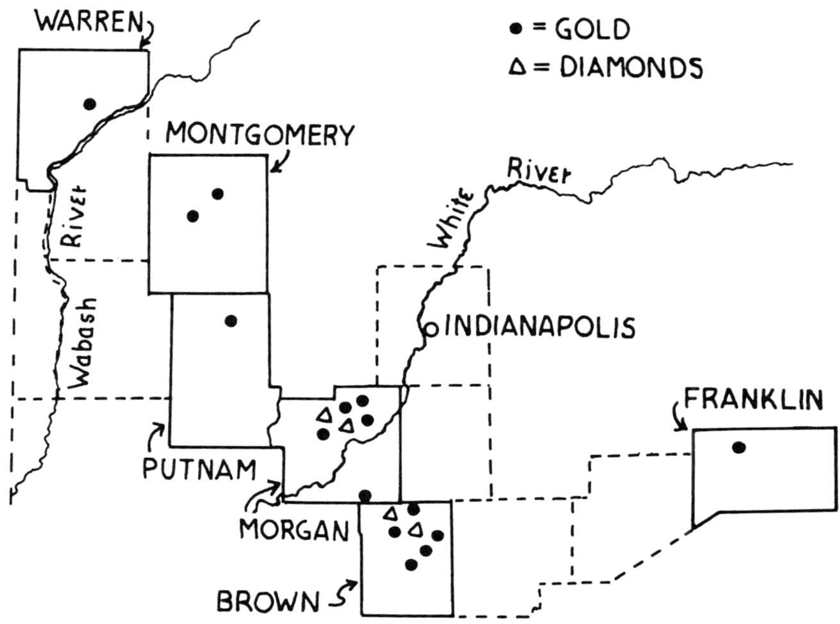

Locations in Central Indiana for gold and diamonds

west. Outcrops along streams in the county may reveal pyrite or gypsum as well as fossils. A small stream with pyrite is a mile and three-quarters northwest of Salem. A cut in the spillway of a dam 2 miles south of Salem on Indiana 135 has yielded barite, quartz, and sphalerite.

Monroe County has geodes and numerous minerals. Road cuts near Bloomington expose barite, siderite, apatite, goethite, quartz, calcite, and sphalerite. Any new road cut or excavation should be investigated. Productive cuts have been both north and south of Bloomington on Indiana 37. Road cuts on Highway 37 north and south of Harrodsburg have crystals. Abandoned quarries yield specimens of dolomite, barite, quartz, glauconite, marcasite and more with one being 1/2 mile east of Unionville on Indiana 45. Another is 1 mile west of Smithville and a third is 2-3/4 miles west of Smithville. A fourth is 1 mile north of Harrodsburg on the west side of the road.

Stream cuts in Monroe County are also productive. Two of the streams are Clear Creek south of Harrodsburg 11/4 miles, and Griffys Creek 1 mile north of Bloomington. Fluorite and sphalerite are found on the stream by the University Reservoir.

Salem limestone is very fossiliferous. Some of the fossils such as Endothyra, a calcareous shelled protozoan are microscopic, but other marine creatures, corals, snails, clams, moss animals, sea lilies, lamp shells and more are plainly visible.

One of the virtues of this stone is that it is uniform and compact so that it can be cut in any direction. Thick layers can be cut into enormous blocks. Several thousand people are employed in the limestone industry and millions of dollars worth of high grade stone are produced each year. Exposures of this limestone are in Lawrence County, Monroe County, and Washington County, and a few places as far south as the Ohio River.

Mississippian fossils are to be found in the Salem limestone so that numerous snails make an ornamental pattern in the stone in some areas, while in others "Indian beads" crinoid stem sections provide unusual patterns.

A well-known site in Washington County is the railroad cut through Spergen Hill east of Salem and 2.7 miles west of South Boston on Indiana Highway 160. Turn north here on the secondary road and go 1/2 mile north.

There are four miles of Ordovician fossil exposures along Elkhorn Creek south of Richmond between Liberty Pike and Indiana Highway 227. Liberty Pike crosses Elkhorn Creek 5 1/2 miles south of Richmond,. Highway 227 is about 2 miles southeast of South Richmond in Wayne County. Fossils are also found north of Brookville on the east side of the highway.

A favorite fossil area is the river bluffs near Madison. The Ordovician marine fossils occur in road cuts along Indiana Highway 7 where the road climbs the Ohio River bluff northwest of Madison in Jefferson County. Other exposures are in cuts along Highway 62 west of Madison opposite the power plant. The rock strata with the honeycomb coral masses is productive. An excellent area is along the railroad cuts west of Highway 7, providing a scenic area for fossil collectors.

Road cuts along Indiana 56, 3 miles south of Rising Sun, Ohio County, have many species of well-preserved Ordovician marine fossils. The cuts are on the right side of the highway as it goes up the bluff of the Ohio River.

Three miles west of Peppertown in western Franklin County there are numerous Ordovician fossils weathering from the shaley limestone. Take the secondary road northwest of Peppertown 1.7 miles to a series of junctions. Keep to the left at the first junction, then turn right and cross Salt Creek, then keep left. Turn right after 0.8 mile and stop at the fossiliferous roadcut on the right.

Silver Creek in Union County is a location for corals, lamp shells and moss

Fossils are found in road cuts north of Brookville, south of Richmond and along the creek between Route 27 and 227

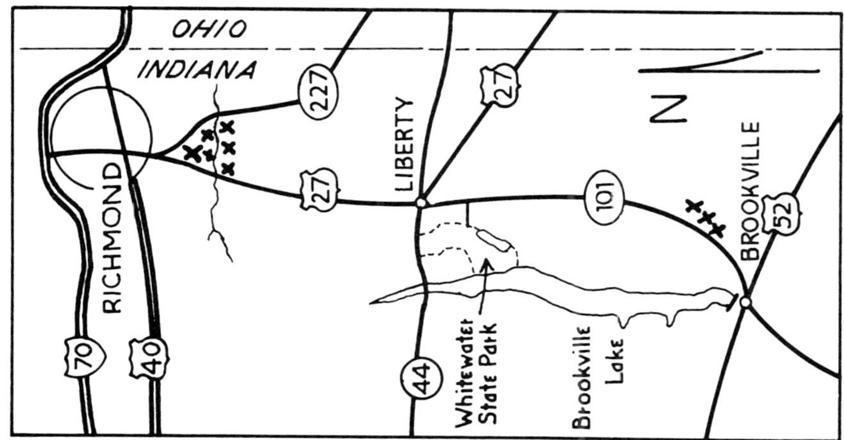

animals. The creek is 1/2 mile west of Liberty on Highway 40 and then left on a secondary road which crosses Silver Creek. After crossing the creek turn north at the intersection and park.

A location for the fascinating hishi-like Indian beads of the Mississippian Period is on Indiana 46, 7 miles east of Bloomington. The disc-shaped sections of the crinoids or "sea lilies" are popular with children and serve to interest them in geology. The small discs are about 1/4 to 3/8 inch in diameter and have knurled edges with center holes having various geometric shapes.

Another "Indian bead" location is 1 1/2 miles south of New Ross in Montgomery County. The old quarry is on Racoon Creek. Dump piles there are fossiliferous shale.

Indiana quarries are private property so be sure to ask for permission. Stay away from the edges of old quarries which are filled with water.

A highlight for collectors in southern Indiana is the Corydon area of Harrison County. The Corydon Quarry at the northwest edge of the city is a fruitful place to look for sharply chiseled crystals of fluorite, calcite and quartz. Access to the quarry has been granted on weekends. Excellent fluorite crystals have also been found 5 miles west of Corydon and 1 mile west of Corydon in road cuts on Indiana Route 62. A possibility of finding aragonite and dolomite specimens is here too. Another quarry is 2 1/2 miles south of Lanesville in the eastern part of the county. The Corydon area dolomite crystals are well-known among collectors because they are lustrous, well-formed, and have a delicate pink tint.

Geodes are found in Floyd County southwest of Edwardsville and in the eastern part of Clark County. Clark County is noted for Devonian corals and other fossils. Exposures can be found along the Ohio River and north of Carwood in road cuts and stream banks. Fossils are abundant in Dearborn County. Look for these Ordovician fossils in road cuts and stream banks near Guilford, Weisburg, and west of Lawrenceburg.

In Warrick County, coal seams reveal plant fossils with exotic leaves and strange woods from ancient forests. Exposures are north of Boonville on

The Corydon Quarry location in Harrison County

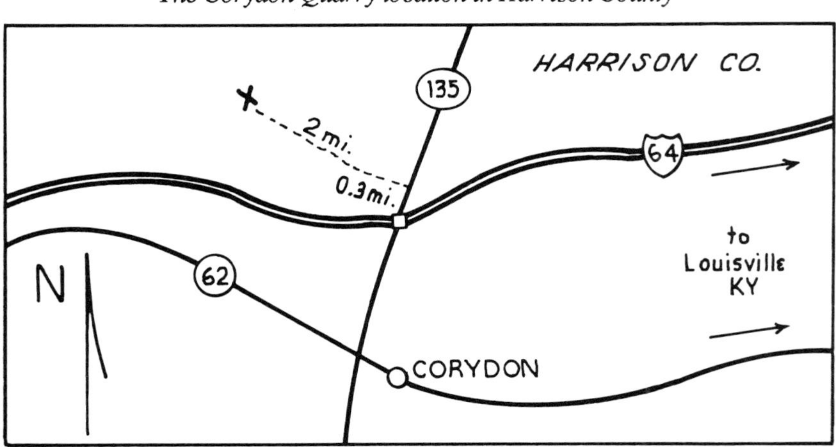

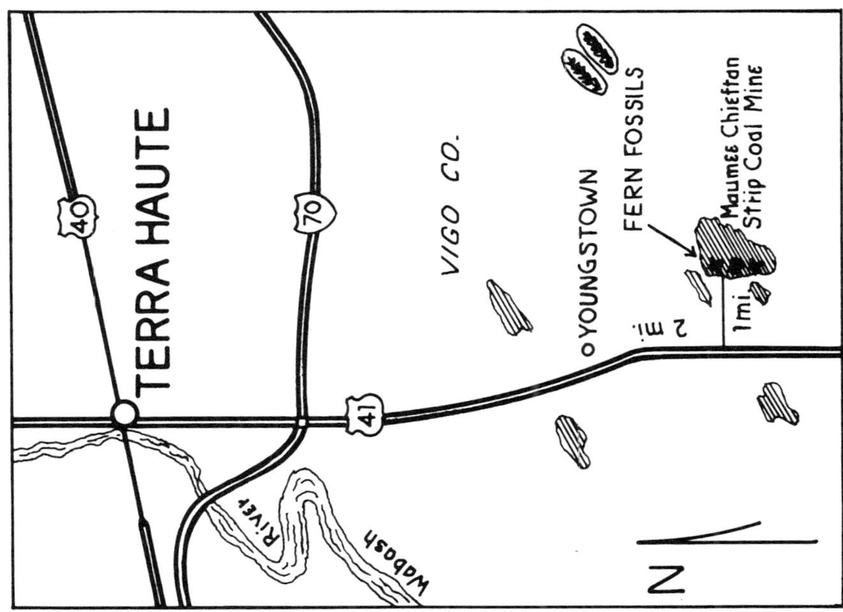

Highway 51. Marine fossils can be found between Yankeetown and Scalesville. Mississippian fossils are abundant at Ray's Cave at Ridgeport.

Perhaps the most collectable of Indiana's plant fossils are the "fern fossil" concretions of Vigo County found near Terre Haute. The tan and gray oval-shaped concretions of the local coal mines have perfectly preserved remnants of coal age flora. There are distinct ferns, reeds, mosses, leaves, and bark prints of long extinct vegetation, all to be seen only after carefully opening the concretions by splitting them. Plant fossil imprints are also seen on the shale associated with the coal.

In Vigo County near Terre Haute, collectors have found excellent Pennsylvanian fossils at Fowler Park, south of the beach. The park is east of U.S. 41, just south of the city. Follow the park signs at the Stuckey store corner. These fossils are also exposed along the road south of Youngstown.

There are also strip mines in Sullivan County where plant fossils are exposed along the sides of the mines south of Dugger. At the junction of Indiana 162 and Indiana 64 in Dubois County east of Huntingburg there are outcrops of Mississippian fossils.

A quarry at Norristown in Shelby County on Indiana 9 has calcite, fluorite and pyrite in addition to a variety of Silurian fossils. Look also for Silurian fossils along Big Blue and Flat Rock Creeks in the same county.

On Indiana Route 101 in Franklin County north of Brookville and in the Whitewater valley are outcrops of Ordovician fossils including trilobites, brachiopods and corals.

In southeastern Indiana in outcrops west of Madison on Indiana 162 near the railroad cut there are several species of Ordovician fossils.

For collecting fossils in Indiana you should have a cold chisel in addition to your geologists hammer. A strong knife and several sizes of screw drivers are also handy. The fossils may be molds, casts, pieces of shell, carbonized leaves, pyrite pseudomorphs, silica replacements, or microfossils in limestone. The finest specimens can be collected from weathered rocks in abandoned quarries, stream beds, disintegrating banks, road cuts, railroad cuts and recent excavations.

Although esthetic fossils from Indiana are featured displays in many museums, the fossils have more importance than merely being ornamental. Paleontologists and geologists study the history of earth and life forms of the past by examining fossils and much of this study sheds light on ecological and environmental problems of today. Fossils indicate the age of the rock in which they are found and tell what kind of world was present in this area at a given time and the relationship of different parts of the world in the past. Fossils are also valuable in prospecting for natural resources; for example, Pennsylvanian fossils are an indication of coal, beds and Foraminifera are of assistance when looking for oil.

Foraminifera are common in Indiana limestone, especially in Mississippian rocks. Stromotoporoids are abundant in coral reefs of Indiana. Ordovician and Silurian corals of many species are present. Excellent bryzoans are common in the streams and gullies of scenic southeast Indiana. Some of the finest bryzoans in the country are found here. Archimedes, the screw-shaped bryzoan, is highly prized.

Southern Indiana also has widespread brachiopods, being plentiful at Jefferson Lake, for example. Brachiopods lived attached to the sea floor or to the shells of other marine animals. They differ greatly in shape and size from1/2 inch or less to 2 inches and over. A line drawn down through the center of the beak to the bottom of the shell will yield two symmetrical halves. Many are ridged, some are smooth, and others have delicate spines. Brachiopods are the most common of all invertebrate fossils in Indiana, being especially abundant in southeastern Indiana, sometimes in beds as much as 2 feet thick.

Fossil plants are found in southern Indiana sandstone. Indiana Geological Survey photo

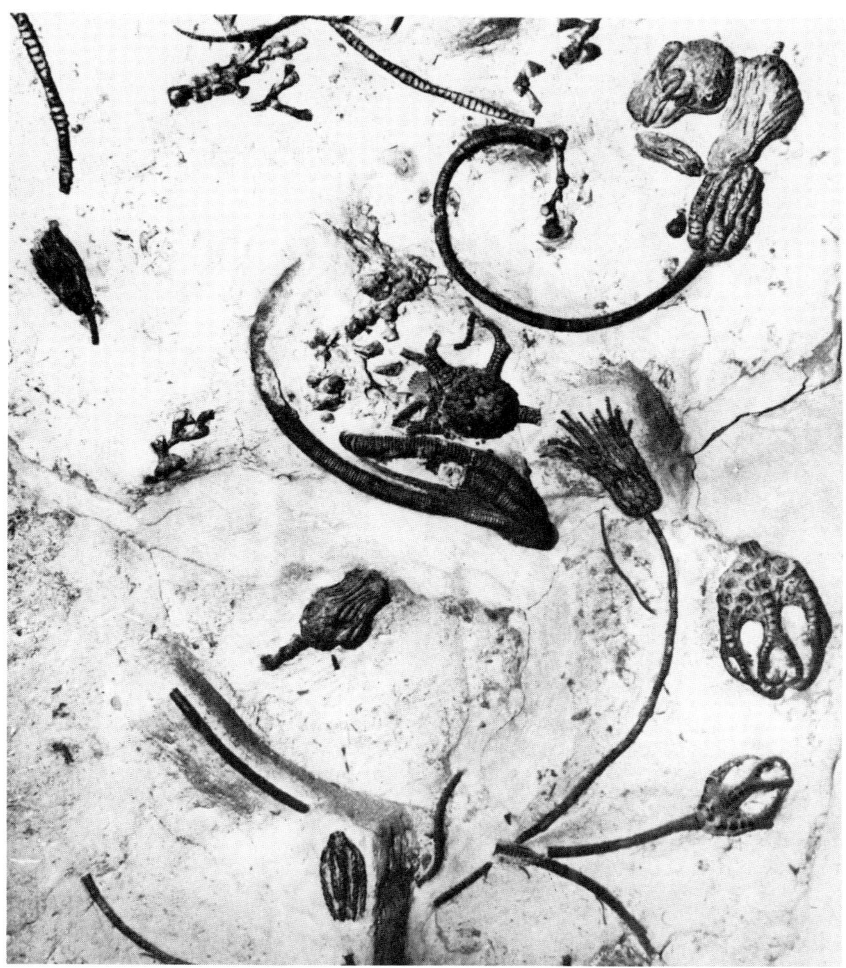

Crinoids, often called "sea lilies", are a primary goal of fossil hunters. Indiana Geological Survey photo

Phylum Mollusca is well represented by many pelecypods and gastropods, or clams and snails as they are commonly called. The pelecypods are rare in most strata of Indiana except for the Ordovician, but the sturdy snails are found in most strata and are very abundant in Salem limestone.

The Nautiloids, free-swimming mollusks with curved, straight, or tightly coiled shells, are common in Hoosier rocks of the Ordovician and Silurian Periods.

Trilobites, belonging to the Arthropods, are all extinct but, for collectors, are a major goal in this state. Isotelus, Dalmanite, and Calymene are some of the favorites, along with the best known of this class, Phacops rana. Look for trilobites in Ordovician, Devonian and Silurian formations.

Starfish, blastoids, crinoids, and other echinoderms are also much

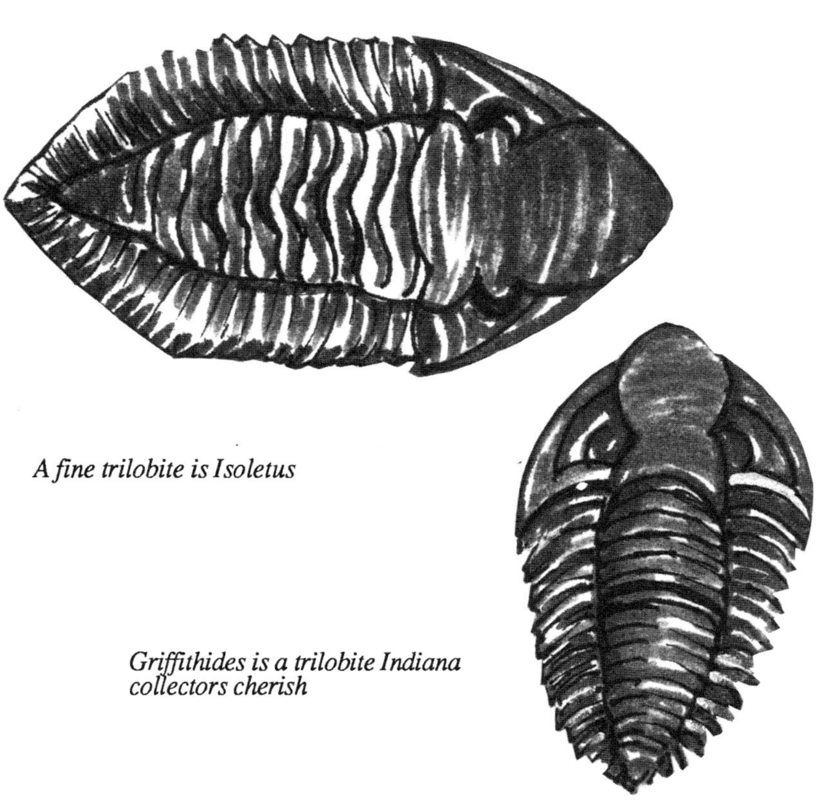

A fine trilobite is Isoletus

Griffithides is a trilobite Indiana collectors cherish

desired Hoosier fossils. Magnificent crinoids have been found near Crawfordsville and various Mississippian quarries, and the stems occur in limestone of the Ordovician, Silurian and Devonian Periods.

There are several caves in Crawford County, the best known being Marengo Cave northeast of Marengo and Wyandotte Cave, just east of Wyandotte. Calcite, aragonite, gypsum and dolomite are found in road cuts and banks near the caves. The dolomite cut is on Indiana 62, 1/4 mile east of Wyandotte. Aquarry on the northwest edge of Milltown has dolomite and fluorite.

A quarry in Perry County, 1/2 mile east of Branchville, has crystals of gypsum, calcite, aragonite, and marcasite. Barite is found at another quarry 1 mile northeast of Derby, while fossils are exposed along Anderson Creek and in road cuts near the Ohio River.

Indiana collectors are always aware of the gold and diamonds found in the state. Some of the diamonds were found while prospectors were panning for gold and were white, pink, greenish-yellow, light yellow, and light brown. Some of the crystals were too small to cut, but the largest crystal, named Stanley, was about 5 carats and was cut into two stones.

Morgan and Brown Counties were the leading producers of diamonds and gold, but gold has also come from streams in Vanderburgh County,

Gibson County, Pike County, Warren County, and Putnam County. The gold is found in magnetite sands and is accompanied by nuggets of copper, galena, pyrite, hematite, limonite, flakes of mica and crystals of several colors of garnets. Rocks of the gold-bearing area are hornblende, schist and gneiss.

In addition to the diamonds and the gold, exquisite pearls have been found in mussels living in clear stretches of the Wabash River, most of which are found between Lafayette and Vincennes.

Dr. Benjamin Moulton of Terre Haute writes that a good place to study the amazing geodes of Indiana is in the prayer garden in back of the Catholic church in Jasper. There was once a monastery here and the residents built the beautiful rock garden with thousands of geodes, many of which were carefully opened to reveal almost every imaginable phase of geode development.

There are earth science collections at Hanover College, Purdue, Indiana University, St. Joseph's, Earlham, and Indiana State. Notre Dame University has a famous American stone mosaic on the campus.

South Bend is known for its impressive shows, and the work of the Evansville Lapidary Society has received much attention. There are 18 excellent clubs in the state and numerous gem and mineral dealers.

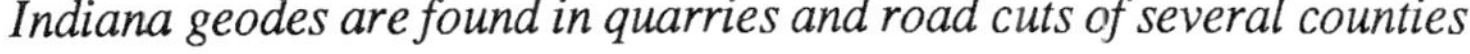

Indiana geodes are found in quarries and road cuts of several counties

Major counties for finding fossils, gems and minerals in Ohio

OHIO

Ohio has suffered more than most states in the loss of collecting sites. Federal Mine Safety and Health regulations have been blamed for the closing of many excellent mines and quarries, but there is more to this loss than MSHA alone since many companies have taken the opportunity of using these regulations as an excuse. Unfortunately, without amateur mineralogists and paleontologists, large chapters of earth's history will be lost through these closed localities.

There have also been changes in ownership from small locally owned quarries to giant multi-interest companies. Another reason for the loss of collecting sites has been vandalism or carelessness. While most such acts involve dropouts and idle young people, some mineral and fossil collectors have hurt the hobby by going in without permission and not obeying the AFMS Code of Ethics.

People have a tendency to sue these days for accidents which are their own fault, so insurance rates have climbed and are especially high for companies which admit the public.

Other problems are the covering over of historic dumps, the immediate replanting of new dumps, and the failure of government and industry to recognize the importance of earth science. If educationally-minded clubs persist in their efforts to reopen lost sites, perhaps there is hope.

Ohio, a highly industrialized state with busy ports along Lake Erie in the north, also has rich farmlands which produce big crops of fruit and vegetables. The many scenic rivers of the state drain into the Ohio, one of the most important rivers east of the Mississippi. Ohio is a leading mineral producer, ranking among the top in the production of limestone, clay, dimension stone, sand, gravel, salt, and crushed stone. The state is a also a leader in the mining of coal and the production of oil and gas. There are some rugged hills in the southeastern part of the state and several sections of the Wayne National Forest. Although not rich in gems, Ohio has plenty of fossils.

Northern Ohio

About 60% of Ohio is glaciated. There are numerous gravel and stone quarries in northern Ohio, prominent in Geauga, Wayne, Stark, Medina and Knox Counties. Glacial gravels can also be seen in stream beds, on terraces, cliffs, road cuts, and excavations. Among the materials found in glacial gravels are granite, porphyry, feldspar, quartzite, quartz, and conglomerate.

One of the best collecting sites in the nation for trilobites, brachiopods and other excellent marine invertebrates was Sylvania in Lucas County. Unfortunately for science, the great quarries are closed to collectors. Some of the exquisitely preserved fossils have been replaced by pyrite. Found in these quarries, in addition to superb large phacops milleri trilobites, were dozens of species of brachiopods, gastropods, bryzoans and corals.

Ottawa County has gypsum at Port Clinton, and at Clay Center, a noted quarry has yielded splendid crystals of celestite, calcite, dolomite and fluorite. It is now closed. Silurian fossils were also found in this quarry and at Genoa in this county.

A location for barite concretions is in Erie County on the Vermilion River. The access is Vermilion Road south to the river about 1 1/2 miles. The concretions are found at the bottom of a steep hill on the north bank to the west of the main road and on either side of the river on a trail to the east. They are abundant at Johnson's Island in Sandusky Bay, at Kelly's Island north of Sandusky, at Marblehead at the end of the peninsula and at the railroad quarry in Venice. A famous celestite quarry is located on South Bass Island.

A real magnet for mineral collectors was the Pugh Quarry, southwest of Bowling Green in Wood County, where superb specimens of celestite, pyrite, fluorite, calcite and barite were collected before the quarry was closed.

Devonian fishes have been found in carboniferous shales near Cleveland, including some unusual specimens with carbonized fins and flesh.

Plant fossils are also found in Pennsylvanian outcrops in northern and northcentral Ohio.

Fossils are abundant in Wyandot and Logan Counties. The Wyandot locations are at Carey and northwest of Crawford. In Logan County, Duff's Quarry north of Huntsville has numerous marine fossils and also fine specimens of calcite and pyrite. Dolomite is also found in this county, and a quarry at East Liberty has both crystals and fossils. Bellefontaine in Logan County is responsible for the first concrete pavement in America. The highest point in the state is Campbell Hill near Bellefontaine, at 1550 feet.

Pyrite crystals from the Duff Quarry at Huntsville in Logan County are exceptional. Some of the iridescent and brilliant crystals are capped with calcite. Six varying crystal habits are found, and some of the crystals appear to be expertly faceted. Other minerals of the Duff Quarry are calcite, dolomite, fluorite and sphalerite.

Central and Southern Ohio

A major collecting area for lapidary material is in Licking and Muskingum Counties and in an adjacent area of Coshocton County. This is the area for finding Ohio's State Gem, its colorful and beautifully patterned flint which is a hard, compact, and fine-grained lapidary material, a variety of quartz, that here grades into chalcedony and agate. Luckily for gemstone enthusiasts, there are several fee basis collecting areas in the flint country, and also collecting is sometimes allowed on other private farms in the area.

There is a State Park at Flint Ridge, where the museum interprets the history and geology of this notable deposit, which was a prime source of

Flint digging areas in Ohio

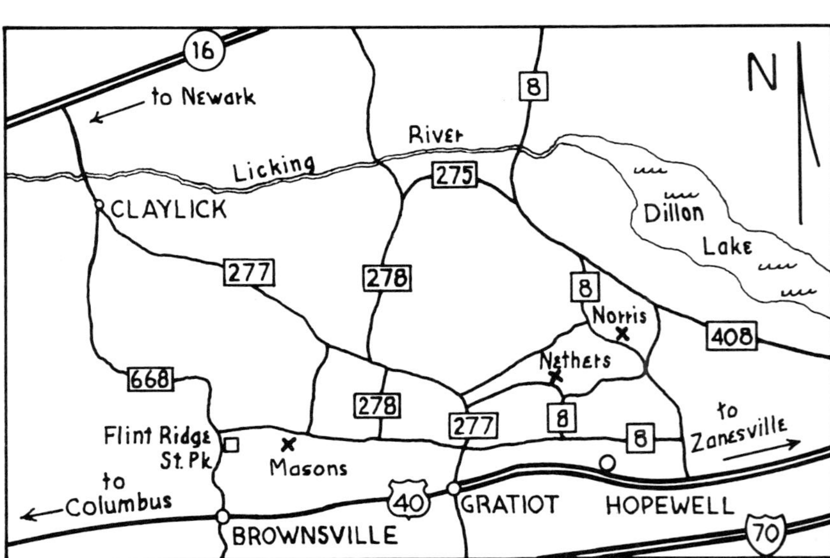

material for projectiles and tools for many Indian tribes. The vast deposit extends from east of Newark in Licking County to Zanesville in Muskingum County.

The flint is impure silica having the hardness of 7, a conchoidal fracture, and uniform texture. It occurs in colors of pink, yellow, gold, orange, rose, red, peach, mauve, blue-gray, rust, brown, beige, ivory, cream, black and white. Patterns resemble clouds, ribbons, flames, waves, and impressionistic scenes. Some flint is spotted, some mottled, and some has translucent bands. Interesting pieces are covered with drusy quartz crystals or have been broken and recemented into solid breccia. According to an expert, the rarest colors are green and lilac, and the rarest pattern is dendritic. Ohio lapidaries have learned to be very selective about the flint they cut, so some of the best finished stones resemble crazy lace agate, flowering jasper, or other fine quartz materials.

Collecting is not allowed in the State Park where the hills are strewn with flint scraps and the flint pits of primitive inhabitants. The places to collect are private property such as Masons House of Flint on Flint Ridge Road near Newark which allows digging. The site is at 15886 Flint Ridge Road S.E., Newark (43056), near the State Park.

Fellowship Farms, the Norris fee site, is located at 4695 Perthill Road, Nashport (43830), which is open all year, weather permitting. Take Perthill Road from Nashport until you reach Sidle Road; Fellowship Farms is at the junction of these two roads.

A superb specimen from the silica shale showing a trilobite, Phacops rana, a crinoid, Arthroscantha, and a bryzoan. Photo courtesy of Black Hills Institute of Geological Research

A well-known flint digging area is the Nethers Farm, 3680 Flint Ridge Road, Hopewell (43746). There are no camping facilities here, although there are at some of the other sites. The digging fee is reasonable and the season lasts from April to mid-November. Sometimes a fully-contained motor home is allowed to stay overnight.

Inquire at the State Museum in Flint Ridge State Park for other collecting areas. Sometimes new areas are added and old ones are dropped or change ownership.

The flint of Coshocton County, north of the flint areas of Licking and Muskingum Counties, is somewhat different. A much admired variety here is called "Nellie Blue" or "Nellie Black" for the small town named Nellie on U.S. 36 east of Coshocton. It is generally darker in color, and the hues tend to be on the cool side of the spectrum instead of the lighter, brighter colors of Flint Ridge. There are many shades and tints of blues, grays, and blacks forming striking patterns in the hard fine-grained material. The flint deposit is south of Nellie with access to the area from State Highways. There is often a fee digging area there. Inquire locally for directions to either the Clark Farm or the Sells Farm.

Ohio flint dates from the Pennsylvanian Period and is found in layers from 3 miles southeast of Newark to 12 miles northwest of Zanesville where the main deposits cover a distance of over 8 miles. It is geologically defined as chert, a compact siliceous chalcedonic mineral of organic or precipitate origin, distributed through limestone beds. Flint, a variety of chert, is uniform, extremely fine-grained and dense, as well as extremely tough. Its smooth, conchoidal fracture distinguishes it from ordinary chert.

The flint deposits are derived from the marine creatures that built up the

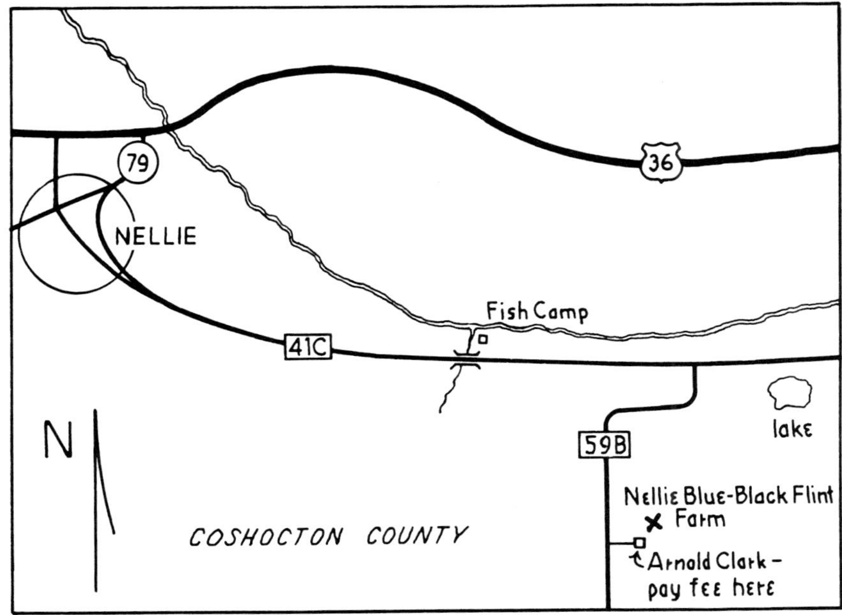

Collecting areas and points of interest to collectors

limestone deposits, which were then infiltrated with silica solutions, converting portions of the limestone beds into chert and flint. In the Ohio flint regions, the material is 98% pure silica, 2% water, with trace amounts of iron, manganese and other coloring agents. Averaging about 6 feet in thickness, the beds vary from 1 to 10 feet thick. In the flint beds are many forms of cryptocrystalline and crystalline quartz.

Hundreds of old pits are exposed over the whole area, some quite shallow and some at considerable depths. Besides this historic region, the many Ohio Mounds are of great interest to visitors.

In selecting flint for polishing, Ohio lapidaries avoid that which appears porous. They look first for good color and pattern, and then for density, smooth fracture, and translucency at thin edges. The toughness and uniformity of flint allows you to cut elaborate shapes from it, the same qualities which made original Americans choose it for blades, drills, knives, spades, celts, axes and projectile points. It is a good idea to contact a member of an Ohio club before making a trip for flint. The Licking County Rock and Mineral

Society is in Newark, where Helen Smith, bulletin editor, has frequent flint reports. Other clubs near the flint region are at Columbus and Mansfield.

There are also fossils in the flint region. Pelecypods and brachiopods are found at Granville, Newark (2 miles south at Bald Knob) and Flintridge in Licking County. In Muskingum County pelecypods are found at Adams Mills and New Concord.

Fossils are found in the central part of the state in the Columbus vicinity. Devonian invertebrates are found in the State Quarries. Other fossiliferous quarries are at Hayden Falls and Marble Cliff. On the Franklin County line, brachiopods and other fossils are abundant in the Devonian limestone west of Harrisburg on Big Darby Creek.

Trilobites and other fossils are found in Greene County. Dolomite and more fine crystals were found west of Jamestown. A mineral collector from Springfield found a scarce crystal of pyrrhotite at a quarry near Cedarville.

On Caesars Creek in Warren County southwest of Waynesville, horn corals, crinoids, brachiopods, and trilobites are found. Miami Valley Mineral and Gem Club members found a polishable fossiliferous limestone here too. Collecting is on both sides of the creek in the Flood Control Zone. Take Clarksville Road 1 mile south of Waynesville and then go west to the Reservoir. Hunt along the spillway or cross the dam and hunt about 600 yards southeast. Ask for additional information at the Engineer's Office or at the Visitors Center on Clarksville Road near the dam.

Fossils are found east of Camden in Preble County. In Butler County is Hueston Woods State Park. Collecting is permitted for the numerous Ordovician fossils here. The attractive park, near Oxford, provides camping facilities. Gravel is also produced in this county.

There are fossils near Blanchester in southern Clinton County. These are Ordovician trilobites, pelecypods and brachiopods.

Calcite crystals come in fascinating colors and forms and are found throughout the Midwest

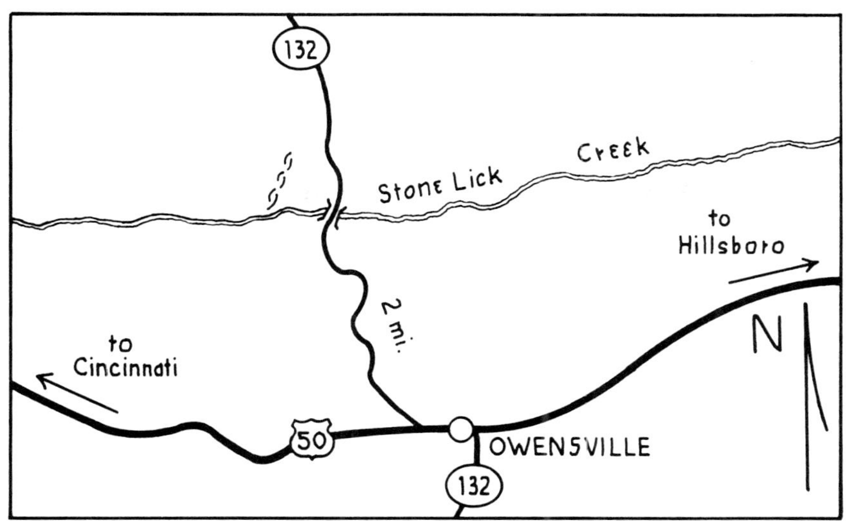

An Ohio site for placer gold is on Stone Lick Creek

In Ross County near Bainbridge. there is a location for cone-in-cone calcite, concretions and geodes which are locally called cannon balls. The geodes weather from a high hill overlooking Paint Creek. Take Route 50 east of Bainbridge to Jones Levee Road and turn south to Spargersville Road. Turn west here, until a dead end side road turns north. Follow this trail to the creek. This is another area visited by the Miami Club.

In the Cincinnati area, Ordovician fossils are abundant in road cuts, stream banks, and excavations. There are bryzoans, crinoids, and pelecypods.

Chert, dolomite and Silurian fossils come from Highland County. A good location is near Hillsboro where many road cuts expose good fossils. Geodes are reported in Highland County 5 miles south of Marshall.

Fine-grained chert is present in Adams County 1 mile southwest of Jacksonville and south of the bridge.

Ohio hobbyists have enjoyed panning for gold in several places in the state and have often come up with colors and flakes, even tiny nuggets, in their pans. Stonelick Creek north of Owensville in Clermont County is a spot for this activity. Both the Newark Club and the Miami Valley Club have shared directions with other hobbyists. Owensville is several miles east of Cincinnati on Highway 50. Turn north at Owensville on Highway 132 until you cross the bridge over Stonelick Creek, turn right at the first road on the north side of the bridge and park along the stream. This is private property, so get permission.

Conglomerate and flint are found in Hocking County. The flint is 2 1/2 miles southwest of Kachelmacher. The conglomerate is in Hocking State Park. There are also outcrops of sandstone in this scenic park. Harold McClure, Ohio State Director for the Federation, gives a selenite location in this county. On Route 93, 5 miles north of Logan is the Webb Summit sign.

Turn left at the first road where there is a "no outlet" sign, drive to the stop sign at the top of the hill. Watching out for small aircraft, turn right on the gravel runway and look for mounds of clay 200 to 500 feet from the stop sign. Do not park on the runway. There is selenite on the surface and not more than a foot deep. Some attractive crystals may be found. The driveway is locked at 2:00 PM on Saturdays.

There is a flint deposit in Vinton County west of Prattsville. Pelecypods and other fossils are common in the black carbonaceous Pennsylvanian shales.

Another flint location is in Lawrence County at Pine Creek and Moulton.

There is great enthusiasm for the rock hobby in Ohio and the clubs urge visitors to help keep the places open where collecting is allowed by heeding the Code of Ethics of AFMS and the Golden Rule. Do not hunt without permission, do not leave gates open, nor drive or park in undesignated areas, and leave sites clean, neat and safe for the next group.

A single diamond has been recorded for Ohio, found near Cincinnati in Clermont County in 1897. Pearls have been found in mussels in several rivers in Ohio, the Scioto, Ohio, and Little Miami Rivers being the main ones. Some of the Little Miami River pearls were a delicate pink color.

Ohio has great museums in Cleveland, Columbus, Dayton, Cincinnati, Tiffin and Athens. The annual spring show of the Cincinnati Club is rated as one of the best in the United States. Dayton, Toledo, Mansfield, Columbus, and Berea all have important shows also. There are also numerous mineral and fossil dealers in the state, as well as lapidary manufacturers and suppliers.

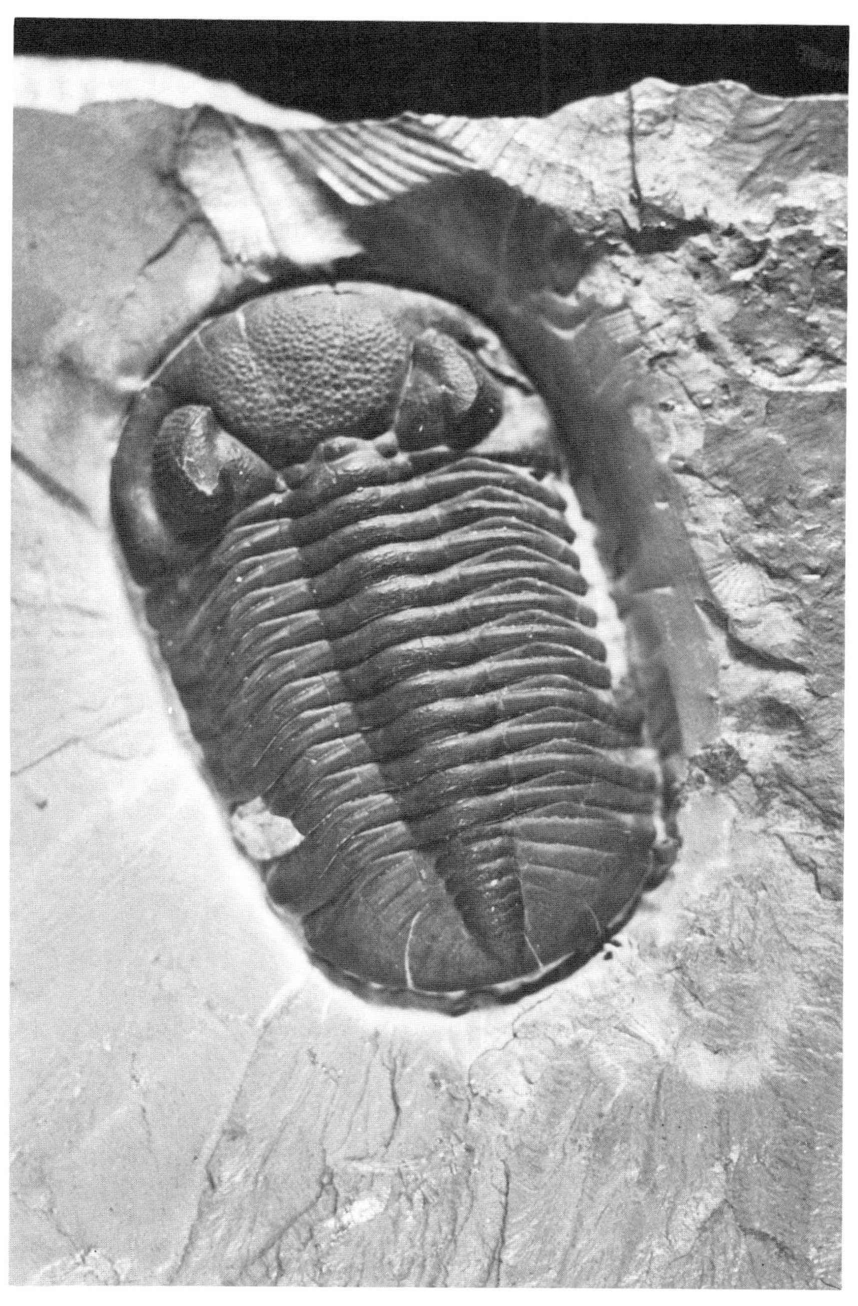

Trilobite Phacops milleri is one of the most sought after Ohio fossils

SUMMARY

Geologically the Midwest is an incredible land, carved by glaciers and situated on the incomparable Great Lakes, the location of the upper Mississippi River valley and the Ohio River. The ancient seas which were once here have helped form the land, and the forests of long ago have left coal deposits. The past has left a legacy to these states of fertile soil, vast resources and splendid scenery.

The copper country of Michigan, the iron ranges of Minnesota, the fluorite area of Illinois, and the limestones of Indiana are unsurpassed. Wisconsin holds great promise for copper, lead, and zinc, and its granite is a national favorite. Ohio, a leading coal producer, has yielded some of the finest fossils ever found. These states are leaders in the production of oil, coal, uranium, salt, granite, sand, gravel, limestone, iron, copper, clay, and gypsum. Diamonds and gold have been found here too; the reserves of minerals are tremendous.

Man has changed the surface of this former wilderness. Forests have been cut down, native plants have been eradicated, potholes have been filled, dams have been built, productive land has been covered by skyscrapers. In this continuing process, important keys to the past have been uncovered, and the mineral and fossil hobbyists have chosen to save this part of our heritage, working with professionals in the true spirit of conservation.

It is true that field trips are not as easy as they used to be. Many do not realize the educational uses to which we put our collections. Major museums display things we have collected, school children study the rocks and fossils we have provided, and scientists write about new species we have discovered.

Lapidaries too have made an important contribution to the arts with beautiful carvings, intricate mosaics, and creative jewelry. We must work on our public relations so that those who help us on our field trips realize that they are helping education, science and art.

This book has given you ideas about where, how, and what to collect, because the thrill of discovery is essential to the growth of our activities. The book has also given you glimpses of the mineral, gem and fossil history of this land. Help make the next edition full of new information, not full of history.

BIBLIOGRAPHY

Minnesota

Wolter, Scott, THE LAKE SUPERIOR AGATE, LSA Inc., 1986

MacFall, Russell, ROCK HUNTERS GUIDE, Crowell, 1980

Ransom, Jay, FOSSILS IN AMERICA, Harper, 1964

Sinkankas, John, GEMSTONES OF NORTH AMERICA, Van Nostrand Reinhold, 1976

Rapp, George and Wallace, D.T., GUIDE TO COLLECTING IN MINNESOTA, U. of Minn., 1979

Wisconsin

MacFall, Russell and Wollin, Jay, FOSSILS FOR AMATEURS, Van Nostrand Reinhold, 1972

Bailey, R.H., GLACIER, Time-Life, 1982

University Research Newsletter, 1977, 78, 79, 80. University of Wisconsin-Madison

Illinois

Simon, Jack A., ROCKS AND MINERALS OF ILLINOIS, Illinois Geological Survey, 1976

Collison, Charles W., GUIDE FOR BEGINNING FOSSIL HUNTERS, Illinois Geological Survey, 1959

Collison, Charles and Skartvedt, Romayne, PENNSYLVANIAN PLANT FOSSILS OF ILLINOIS, Illinois Geological Survey, 1966

Lamar, J.E., INDUSTRIAL MINERALS AND METALS OF ILLINOIS, Illinois Geological Survey, 1969

Frye, John C., INSIDE ILLINOIS, Illinois Geological Survey, 1965

Michigan

Heinrich, Wm. E., THE MINERALOGY OF MICHIGAN, Department of Natural Resources, 1976

Kellsy, Robert W., GUIDE TO MICHIGAN FOSSILS, Department of Natural Resources, 1962

Goldring, Winifred, HANDBOOK OF PALEONTOLOGY FOR BEGINNERS AND AMATEURS, New York State Museum, 1962

Kinne, Russ, LIFE ON A CORAL REEF, Nelson Doubleday, 1961

Clarke, Don H., COPPER MINES OF KEWEENAW, Clarke, 1975

MacFall, Russell, GEM HUNTER'S GUIDE, Crowell, 1975

Poindexter, O.F. et al, ROCKS AND MINERALS OF MICHIGAN, Department of Natural Resources, 1971

Indiana

Erd, R.C. and Greenberg, S.S., MINERALS OF INDIANA, Indiana Geological Survey, 1960

Greenberg, S.S., Bunday, W.M. and McGregor, D.J., GUIDE TO ROCKS AND MINERALS OF INDIANA, Indiana Geological Survey, 1966

Burger, A.M., et al, EXCURSION IN INDIANA GEOLOGY, Indiana Geological Survey, 1966

Blatchley, W.S., GOLD AND DIAMONDS IN INDIANA, Indiana Geological Survey, 1960

Perry, T.G., FOSSILS: PREHISTORIC ANIMALS IN HOOSIER ROCKS, Indiana Geological Survey, 1959

Ohio

Farnsworth, Carolyn, ABOUT OHIO ROCKS AND MINERALS, Ohio Geological Survey, 1962

Stout, Wilber and Schoenlaub, R.A., THE OCCURRENCE OF FLINT IN OHIO, Ohio Geological Survey, 1945

Fenton, C. and Fenton, M., THE FOSSIL BOOK, Doubleday, 1958

MAGAZINES

The Lapidary Journal, 1094 Cudahy, Suite 314, San Diego, CA 92110

Rocks and Minerals, 4000 Albemarle Street N.W., Washington, DC 20016

Rock and Gem, 2660 E. Main, Ventura, CA 93003

Mineralogical Record, 7413 Mowry Place, Tucson, AZ 85741